The Power of One
Can Lead to the
Power of MANY!

Dr. [signature]

GOD'S TRUE LAW

GOD'S
TRUE
LAW

A parent's guide to
raising successful children

GARRETT SOLDANO

NEW YORK

GOD'S TRUE LAW
A parent's guide to raising successful children

ISBN 978-1-61448-350-2 paperback
ISBN 978-1-61448-351-9 eBook
Library of Congress Control Number: 2012944329

Morgan James Publishing
The Entrepreneurial Publisher
5 Penn Plaza, 23rd Floor
New York City, New York 10001
(212) 655-5470 office • (516) 908-4496 fax
www.MorganJamesPublishing.com

Cover Design by:
Rachel Lopez
www.r2cdesign.com

Interior Design by:
Bonnie Bushman
bonnie@caboodlegraphics.com

In an effort to support local communities, raise awareness and funds, Morgan James Publishing donates a percentage of all book sales for the life of each book to Habitat for Humanity Peninsula and Greater Williamsburg.

Get involved today, visit
www.MorganJamesBuilds.com.

Habitat
for Humanity®
Peninsula and
Greater Williamsburg
Building Partner

This book is dedicated to all the people who will apply the teachings they will learn here and change humanity for the better. You are all *true* heroes and I am grateful to serve you. —To you I am indebted.

TABLE OF CONTENTS

PREFACE

It began with a thought....

I looked at my reflection in the mirror one morning shortly after my first son was born and said, *Wow! I'm a Dad!* And then, *Whoa, I'm a Dad!* How fantastic, wonderful, incredible, marvelous, challenging and even a little bit scary that I've been entrusted with the most important job on this earth—being a successful parent. It was, at the same time, exciting *and* sobering.

Sandwiched between the exhilaration of cradling that newborn baby in your arms for the first time and waving goodbye as they leave on their honeymoon or move into their first apartment are the years we have to make sure they are equipped with a solid foundation of values, so whatever they decide to do with their life, they will do it to the best of their ability and with passion. If we do not accomplish this I feel we will have failed as parents.

How many times do we see children fall into patterns of self-destructive behavior like alcoholism, drug abuse, eating disorders, self-esteem issues, relationship & social difficulties or financial problems? Our children are a product of their environment, so as parents we must have a positive influence—not only by how we react to situations and events but also to monitor ourselves constantly in everything that we do and don't do.

With the wealth of knowledge available today there is no excuse not to take action on the debacle we are witnessing with our youth.

For the first time in the history of our species, people are starting to say our children run the risk of not outliving their parents!

Albert Einstein is quoted as having said, "The definition of insanity is doing the same thing over and over again expecting a different result."

It is crucial to take control of our children's actions while they are still young—not when they are leaving for college. As a parent I do not want to find myself thinking back and wondering if I should have done more. I want to be able to look back and know within my heart and soul that I gave my children every opportunity to succeed in this beautiful thing we call life.

MY JOURNEY

As a 14 year old high school freshman, I weighed 152 pounds. Scrawny and skinny didn't begin to describe me. One day, my dad said, "Garrett, what do you want to do after high school?" With chest out and eyes wide open, I replied, "I want to be a Division I football player!" He looked at me and said, "Okay. If that's what you really want, you can do it. I'll do everything I can to help you but it's going to take a lot of commitment and hard work."

With this goal and new found belief in myself, I went to school the next day and told everyone about my plans. I guess I was a little naïve in expecting them to share in my enthusiasm because instead of getting "high fives," most of my friends snickered and I even heard a few say, "You're too little, too short, too slow, too weak, wrong color, go to too small of a high school, etc."

Thank God I had some very influential people in my life to help me resist the negative reactions I got at school. Most importantly, I had the strong support of my mother and my father's unwavering guidance. My dad worked tirelessly, making game films and distributing them to Division I college coaches for their consideration. (We didn't have YouTube back then.) Finally, there was my friend Butch, who was a combination of Arnold

Schwarzenegger and Master Yoda. He was my mentor throughout high school and college. His guidance put "meat on my bones" and planted seeds of success in my mind. These seeds have now grown into flourishing trees that still grow today.

I left everything out on the field during those early days of my football career. I think everybody who knew me would agree and say, "Garrett was a hard worker and had heart."

I knew that if I was going to make it to the Division I level I would have to work ten times harder than everyone around me. I lifted weights before and after football/basketball/baseball practices. I would even work out before varsity basketball and baseball games. Because football took top priority, I guiltily confess that I would miss lay ups or strike out because my arms were made of *Jello* from a chest/back/bicep workout that I had just finished two hours before the game.

During the offseason is when the real work was done. While everybody else was at the lake having a good time, I was doing sprints and drills at the track in the morning, lifting weights with Butch at noon, and topping off the day by running up a steep hill dragging five tires that were tied behind me by a rope attached to my weight belt. This is what my life consisted of for five out of seven days each week.

To go from a skinny 152 pound kid to a Division I linebacker, I knew I had to put on weight. I would consume over 6,000 calories/day. For those of you who are not familiar with counting calories, let me just say that it is a tremendous amount of food. I would be stuffing food into my mouth all day, every day. When I wasn't sleeping, I was eating. Imagine trying to drink a 64 ounce shake made with bananas, peanut butter, ice cream, weight gainer, eggs, safflower oil and protein after you eat a huge Thanksgiving dinner. This is what it was like every day for me.

Oftentimes I would throw up. This was the worst thing imaginable for me because I knew I would have to replace those lost calories. I was like Smeegle in "The Lord of the Rings," infatuated with "my precious" floating in the toilet, but instead of a magical ring it was lost calories.

Many people who knew me in high school will also remember that my constant "sidekick" was a cooler. If I wasn't carrying my "little friend" around with me, you would find it stuffed into my hall locker so I could grab something to eat between classes, or in my gym locker, so I could stuff myself before and after gym class. My life consisted of going to school, working out, eating and playing sports. Don't get me wrong, I still dated and had fun at high school parties and stuff, but only after my workouts and school work were done. I would never miss a workout or skip homework.

Let me elaborate on school. There was one other thing that came before all the workouts, sports, and fun. It was academics. I was in the National Honor Society, Class President during my freshman, sophomore and junior years, and graduated with a GPA over 3.5. My parents had a very simple rule; school before all else and they were adamant about it.

During my high school career, I changed from a 152 pound boy to a 5'11 ¾," 230 pound man. I was 18 years old and I could bench over 315 pounds, squat 600 pounds, leg press over a 1000 pounds and still run a 4.68 40 yard dash. Throughout my three years on varsity I dominated our conference playing linebacker. I was All State and All Conference 2 years in a row. I was voted to numerous Dream Teams and was an All American my senior year.

In February 1996, on National Signing Day, I achieved the goal that had I set out to accomplish three years earlier and signed my letter of intent with Western Michigan University to play football on a full athletic Division I scholarship. Until that time, nobody in the history of my high school had ever achieved that.

Most people would have been satisfied with accomplishing something as big as making it to the Division I level on a full scholarship, but I was not. As soon as I signed with Western Michigan, I had bigger ideas in mind. I wanted to make it to the next level. I wanted a shot at the NFL.

Again, I was told I was too short, not fast enough, not athletic enough, too small of an athletic conference etc. What did I do? I did what I knew best and what worked before. I started my extreme workout regimen all over again. I worked even harder because I knew the talent and competition was going to be much fiercer than playing some local farm boys in a field surrounded by corn.

Throughout college there were some other challenges to contend with. There were injuries, college atmosphere, school, girls etc. I had up years and down years, but by the summer before my last year playing college ball I still had that "ultimate goal" knocking on my door. That summer, I think I worked the hardest I've ever worked. The first game my senior year was against perennial Big 10 Powerhouse, University of Wisconsin, which was ranked number four at the time. We lost a nail biter 19-7. I registered 20 tackles and set the tone for myself for the rest of the season.

By the end of my senior year playing football, I was voted Team Captain, Most Valuable Player and was an All Conference Linebacker. Five years later, I was honored with being voted one of the top 100 football players to ever play at WMU. After the NFL draft of 2001 I was picked up as a free agent with the Chicago Bears. (Even though I was and still am a Lions fan. Chris Speilman was my idol growing up).

Unfortunately, I was cut before training camp. After running around with players at the NFL level, I finally realized it was going to take more than just hard work to make this team. Genetics was going to play a big role. I remember seeing Brian Urlacher, an inside linebacker, running around in practice and I remember thinking, "If that is what a NFL linebacker is, then I don't have a chance."

I did manage to leave my "work ethic" footprint with the Bears and the Strength Coach though. It was during the conditioning drill (600 yard shuttle) against the Free Agent/Draftee Defensive Linemen, Linebackers and Tight Ends. Half way through the test there was nobody within 50 yards of me. I overheard the strength coach screaming, "Would somebody catch him!" Nobody did. Karon, a friend of mine, came up to me gasping and said, "You're like a camel. You can go at a steady pace for long distances, but I am a cheetah and I'm fast over short distances."

I gave him a high five and responded, "You are exactly right."

When I reflect on my experiences, I realize that you have to earn the success, but the lingering question remains, "How does one get the mental drive to want to earn it?" My drive came from the solid foundation my parents built early in my childhood, nurtured by my life experiences, and I am thankful to God for his loving grace throughout my journey. In addition to my parents who were always there encouraging me to strive to be my best, I also had the positive support of some very influential people, like my friend Butch. When you have a strong belief system that says anything is possible if you work hard enough secured firmly in your mind, literally anything *is* possible.

There is no doubt that children change our lives for the better. Nothing can explain the jubilant feeling when meeting your child for the first time. We all remember what it was like to see those beautiful eyes or feel those little hands grasp one of our fingers. One thing is for sure; having children changes our lives in every aspect. I still remember coming home from a five day seminar and changing my son's diaper when he muttered his first word, "Dada" on Father's Day. What a fantastic experience for me as a new parent. Back in the day,

I was the "Cool Guy," (At least, this is how I perceived myself. My wife would probably disagree.) strutting around with nothing but an iPhone strapped to my side. Now, I've morphed into a mixture of "Cool Guy" and "Rambo Dad". The iPhone is still "ready for combat" and strapped and to my right side but it also competes with my satchel (even though my wife calls it a fanny pack on steroids). Along with the satchel, I carry a diaper bag hung over one shoulder [filled with life-saving material in case of a public "dirty bomb"] and in the other arm I am carrying my two year old son, Alex, while trying to keep tabs on my four year old son, Jack. Children definitely do not come with an owner's manual. With this being said, most of us will rely on how we were raised by our parents to parent our own children. I think it is important to take all of the positives out of how we were raised and build upon them. No matter if it was a positive or negative situation. It is our job as parents to build upon our own past experiences so we can pass on good values and parenting to our own children.

I know many people who have had horrible childhoods but they turn it to a positive. This taking of a negative situation and making it positive is what I like to call "resonating high". We do not want to continue to do the same thing over again and expect a different result. Just like Albert Einstein said, that is insanity.

I developed this book to enable parents to not only have the tools to condition their minds for success and abundance, but to pass on solid beliefs to their children. These solid beliefs will lead them to lives of unlimited success filled with prosperity, regardless of occupation. This book is for the parents who want the best for their family.

Who knows if your child will be the next Donald Trump, the next great athlete who takes his or her sport to another level like Muhammad Ali, or the next visionary entrepreneur like Richard Branson? You might be even sitting across the table from the next President of our great nation.

Many people have asked me why I wanted to write this book. My answer to this question can be summed up by a great story about a kid and a starfish. It was originally written by Loren Eisley. It reads as follows:

One day a physicist was walking along the beach after a summer storm. As he was walking he noticed there were thousands of starfish scattered along the beach that were washed up from the high tide. He marveled in the fact that all these star fish were going to dry up and die or become the satisfying dinners of sea gulls.

He shook his head at the waste of life and continued on his journey. As he was walking he looked down the beach and he noticed a young boy picking something up and throwing it into the ocean. He approached the young boy and asked, "Young man, what are you doing?"

The young boy replied, "I'm throwing the starfish back into the ocean. If I don't throw them back, they'll dry up and die, or these stupid birds will eat them."

Backed by all his education and experience the physicist said with confidence, "Don't you realize there are miles and miles of beach and thousands of starfish on the beach? You can't make a difference!"

After listening politely, the boy bent down, picked up another starfish, and threw it back into the ocean. Then, smiling at the physicist, he said, "I made a difference to that one."

Within these pages are *Universal Laws*, which properly applied, will give your child the chance to achieve whatever he or she puts a mind to. I didn't come up with them. These laws have been passed down for generations. My job is to paint a clear picture in your mind and be your guide so you can absorb them and utilize them for your family.

If this book can make a difference in one child's life for the better then I have succeeded. Imagine if I reach ten million children? My vision is to have over ten million parents applying and teaching these laws to their children. This will allow over ten million strong minded future leaders with the right mindset to lead us into the next Golden Age of our species.

Chapter One

AWARENESS

Awareness is empowering.
— **Rita Wilson**

Do you ever wonder why some people attract the same problems repeatedly? They keep having financial problems, bad relationships, weight problems, addiction problems, etc. How many times have we heard, seen, or been a part of a bad relationship? What did you do about these challenges? Did you ever get out from underneath the rock that was holding you down, or was changing hard for you? Are you a person who avoids or despises change? If change comes knocking at the door are you in the corner of the closet with the door shut hoping the "change monster" doesn't find you? How many times have you triumphantly said, "This is the day I will start to change?" As the days and weeks linger by, do you find yourself falling into the same old limiting behaviors and attitudes? How many New Year's resolutions have you made to yourself and after several weeks seen them fall by the wayside?

What about addiction? So many people have some sort of addiction whether it's alcohol, tobacco, drugs, gambling, overeating, sex, porn, excessively working out, shopping, reality TV, work, texting, iPhone, etc. Have you ever wondered why people get sucked into these self-destructive habits?

We all have voids that need to be filled, but do you ever wonder why you will sometimes use destructive behavior to fill these voids? Have you ever wondered what affect this behavior has on your children? How many parents angrily blurt to their child, "You're just like your father/mother." "You never do anything the right way." Or, "You'll never amount to anything." Do you think this makes a lasting impression in your child's mind? You bet it does!

Have you ever heard of the sayings, "You become what you think about most," "You become your thoughts," or "Your focus is your reality"? The *Law of Attraction* says everything that has happened in your life both good and bad was attracted to you through your consistent thoughts.

This will get the ego in some of you all fired up but it is true. In this book I will explain why you keep walking down your path of destructive behavior and why you keep attracting the same challenges in your life, whether it's money problems, weight loss, relationship problems, not living a passionate life, negativity, etc.

Speaking of negativity, have you ever been around someone who is always pessimistic? I was talking to a young lady about being negative and I asked her why she was so downbeat about everything. We could be talking about a beautiful sunny day and she'd immediately add a negative comment like, "It's too hot, the sun causes cancer, or it's supposed to storm next week."

Her explanation was one that was rooted in fear. She was afraid to get her hopes up and then be disappointed. Wallowing in the negative negated the possibility of being let down. Unfortunately, this is not how the universe works and she never figured out why she kept having negative things "mysteriously" show up in her life on a continuing basis. You will learn why this happens in this book.

Where do we learn our behavior? Initially, most of us mirror the behavior of our parents and if our parents aren't in the equation then we mirror anything else in our immediate environment. You need to understand and grasp this concept in order for you to start making changes in yourself. Once you are aware of your own destructive behavior then you can monitor yourself so you don't contaminate your children's minds.

If you have ever read any of his books or watched the TV shows starring world renowned dog trainer, Cesar Millan, you will see him work wonders with animals and their owners. Coming into a situation where a dog is out of control, timid, aggressive, suffering from high anxiety, etc., he will initially just observe the situation. Usually, the common denominator in most cases is that the owner(s) has not established themselves as being the "pack leader". This allows the dog to control the situation. Once he brings this awareness to the owner, Cesar will teach the owner how to be the "pack leader". In most cases there is a complete turnaround in the owner and dog's behavior. Everybody wins.

How many times have you gone shopping to the mall or grocery store and seen *those parents* who obviously are not the pack leaders, thereby allowing their children to "run the show." Just the other day I saw two young boys literally running around and screaming while they were tearing things off the shelf and throwing them at each other. During the "carnage" came empty threats from the parents. You could tell there was never any follow through with discipline because there wasn't a moment of hesitation when little "Jimmy" threw one of the boxes of mac and cheese at his parent. The kids were controlling the strings and the puppets, I mean parents, were the ones dangling down below. Are you one of *those parents*? Just like Cesar, this book will teach you how to be the "pack leader" in your family and allow you to build foundations of not only great behavior but solid beliefs, which will allow your children to further society and not inhibit it.

When you understand and are aware of why you keep attracting the same problems to your environment—whether it is debt, bad relationships, undisciplined children, addictions etc. — you then can utilize and train the most important tool in your body, that is, your mind. Once you can effectively exercise and control your own mind you will be able to start the process of conditioning your children's minds. I'm not going to give you fish. I am going to teach you how to fish. Then, in time, you will teach *your* children how to fish.

When you look back at your past, where *were* you? What were you like as a person or parent? Did you have hopes and dreams? Did you have hopes and dreams for your child? What types of friends did you surround yourself with? Who did your children hang out with? Did you have goals and aspirations to look forward too?

If I were to jump into my *Back to the Future* Delorean (For those of you who have never seen the 80's classic, rent it immediately along with *Goonies, Weird Science, Can't Buy Me Love* and all the other 80's classics.) and visit "you" in the past and ask this very simple question, "Where are you going to be in the future?" what would you have told me? Are you today where you wanted to be back then?

Maybe an even more important question to ask would be, "How are you going to live *now* in order to create a tomorrow you will be passionate about? What's important to you now and what will be important to you in the future?"

You must seize the moment. "Carpe Diem"! Seize the day! In the future you will be looking back at today, like you are now looking back at yesterday, last year or 10 years ago. Will you be happy when you look back or will you be sad? Will you be grateful or ungrateful?

Will you feel like you're on top of the world or in your own deep dark lonely hole of mediocrity?

When you look back at your past, do you experience the negative emotions of tragedy, regret, worry, frustration, anger or feel you've been or cheated? I know I did. What did you do about it? Did you rise above and grab the rope out of your own hole of mediocrity or did you suppress it all and lay stagnant in your own pool of self-pity having a glass of "It's everybody else's fault"?

The most powerful way to shape our lives is to get ourselves out of this hole of mediocrity by taking the rope and climbing out. We must take action. You have to MOVE. Different actions produce different results. Why? Because every action is a cause set in motion. These effects will build on past effects (the *Universal Law of Cause and Effect*) to move us in a definite direction…our true destiny.

Now, I congratulate every single one of you for taking the action to read this book. It took some sort of effort, no matter how minimal, to purchase and read this book. Let me ask you this. Are there others who took some kind of action not to buy the book? That is to say, they went online or to the bookstore and decided that it wasn't for them and did not purchase the book?

We have two different people starting in the same position and you chose door number one and bought the book. They chose door number two and decided not to purchase the book. Different actions produce different results.

This means the person who chose door number one will now have the knowledge of the mind to further not only themselves, but everybody in their environment. The person who chose door number two may continue to wander around in what I call "The Fog" of their mind. We will get into "The Fog" later, but "The Fog" is the 99% of the people will choose to conform to their environment rather than to change it for the better. Not only will they remain in "The Fog", but they will not have the proper tools to further their children's "prosperity" this time around and history may repeat itself over and over again.

How many people do you know who have chosen door number two and continue to be in "The Fog" of the mind? You probably do not have to look far to find them. What's worse is we don't have to look far to see a bad example of a parent. It's frustrating—especially when those bad parents are in your family or close friends.

Actions that people decide to take in their lives build on past actions and move them toward a definite direction. It is like building a brick road to an end result. With each action you lay down another brick that furthers your journey toward your ultimate destination or destiny. Your destiny can be great or mediocre. It can further society or inhibit it. You can change people's lives or you can bring them down. It depends entirely on the types of bricks (actions) you are willing to lay down toward your destiny.

How do we know what kind of bricks to lie down on the path to our true destiny? We use the power of decision. The decisions you make right now will shape who you are and who you become. In these moments of decision, your true path will be revealed and you will be on your own journey to your true destiny.

The most unbelievable thing about this power is that it's available to you now as you read these written words. Look into your heart, look into your soul. Right now you can stand up and claim this power, which has transcended throughout time and molded and shaped human destiny. You merely have to muster the courage to claim it. Now is the time to design not only your future, but also to lay down a solid foundation that will enable your children to live a life full of abundance in every aspect of their lives. If you decide not to live a life full of abundance then you've made a decision haven't you? Either way it is a decision. You can decide to claim this power or decide to not to.

Before utilizing your decision making powers, you will utilize something even more "magical"—your thoughts. If the big brother of "action" is "the power of decision" then "actions" and "the power of decision's" father is your "thoughts". Everything begins with a thought. When you decide what to do with that thought then you can take the necessary actions to accomplish the thought—"do or do not there is no try." (Master Yoda).

If you utilize the magical power of your consistent thoughts then you will experience a life full of abundance. What does the word "abundance" mean anyway? *Dictionary.com* defines it this way: *"Abundance is an extremely plentiful or over sufficient quantity or supply of overflowing fullness."*

Let me ask you this, "Do you think God* wants you to have abundance? Do you think He wants you to have an over sufficient quantity or supply of overflowing fullness?"

You bet He does! God wants us to be prosperous in all aspects of our lives. We have to come to this conclusion in our minds if we [and our children] are to live a more abundant life. If we decide not to accept this as truth, we will continue to live a limited life and in turn pass on this limited life to our children. We will continue to walk around in "The Fog" of our mind holding the hands of our children.

"The Fog" encompasses the 99% of the people around us that just do enough to get through in life. People who are in the fog are like programmed robots that allow their current environment to continuously program them blindly and allow their own ego (more on ego later) to dictate their lives.

---

* People will always try to simplify what God is so we can relate to Him. Most of the time, when we perceive God in our minds we see a man with a long white beard surrounded by puffy white clouds. To me God is so much more. God is the spiritual source of all life, an Infinite Being, which is greater than the universes He created. The spiritual concept of God uses terms like immanent, omnipotent, omniscient and transcendent to express this idea of an infinite consciousness and wisdom. When we perceive God in this expansive point of view, we will see that He is greater than all manifestation and yet is aware of every part of that manifestation.

Abundance is not hiding underneath a rock or in a pit full of molten lava. It has been around you your whole life. You just weren't aware of how much of God's abundance is surrounds you. Let me show you how much abundance is out there.

Have you ever been to the beach? Have you ever picked up a handful of sand and marveled at the fact that you probably were holding thousands of sand particles in your hand? Now take the beach you were standing on. Take all the beaches in the world. What about all the deserts in the world. Pretty overwhelming isn't it?

What about the night sky? How many stars make up the universe? Estimates range from 32 followed by 21 zeros to an infinite amount. Let's just write out that number— 32,000,000,000,000,000,000,000. Boggles the mind doesn't it?

Have you ever wondered how many drops of water are in a glass of water? What about the number of rain drops in a summer thunderstorm? What about in a lake? What about the Mississippi River? How many drops of water are in all the oceans of the world?

You really do not have to go far to experience God's abundance. All you have to do is look at yourself in the mirror. The person you see in the reflection is a part of God. Unfortunately, many people do not take advantage of this beautiful gift we see in the mirror every day.

Have you ever really thought about what you are made of? Did you know you have approximately 100 trillion cells that make up your body? All those cells started with the division of one single cell. That single cell, which had the same structure as all the cells in your body now, came from the union of your mother's egg cell and your dad's sperm cell. Let this sink into your mind. Your father's microscopic sperm had to travel a distance of 3-4 inches to achieve its destination and fertilize the egg. For that tiny little cell to travel those few inches would be like you running a 26 mile marathon to achieve your goal! It wasn't like this tiny sperm didn't have competition either. It had to compete and fight with over 280 million other sperms that are willing to die to achieve the goal of arriving and fertilizing the grand prize, your mother's egg. This dedication, this drive, this miracle is what made you. Can you imagine going up against 280 million people and trying to win a race? What you are made up of did…and won. You are the definition of a winner. You must believe this every time you look in the mirror. We all are very special. We all are survivors. You must resonate how miraculous you really are and have this awareness in order to solidify this new abundant belief system in your mind so you can start living a life full of passion and be able to pass this abundant belief to your children.

This book will allow you to have a clear picture in your mind on how to tap into this abundance. You will learn to be grateful when you accept it without fear, guilt and other negative emotions that have been programmed into not only your mind but your genetic makeup—even down to the cellular level. You are probably thinking right now, "What in the heck do my cells have to do with how much success I attract in my life and how I parent?" It has everything to do with it!

Everything in the universe is energy. Energy exists everywhere and when in motion it creates an energy field allowing energy to be absorbed, conducted and transmitted. All objects, including your body, radiate, absorb and conduct frequency waves of energy. Our bodies may appear to be solid but if we magnified our cells, molecules, and atoms, we would see that we are made up of small energy fields vibrating at a certain frequency. You have to remember we are not physical beings living a spiritual existence, but spiritual beings living a human experience. This spiritual energy is what we are composed of. If you take an "alive you" and a "dead you," there really isn't a difference in the matter that makes up your body. That is to say, the alive you and dead you both have two ears, two eyes, nose, mouth, heart, lungs, skin, etc. The only thing missing is this life force, your energy.

These energy forces within us can penetrate everything and cause instantaneous reaction at incredible distances. In mathematics, the *Chaos Theory* explains this further using the example of *The Butterfly Effect*. It states that the flapping of a butterfly's wings represents a small change in the environment that can influence large phenomena in distant places if they are sensitive to their initial conditions. For example, a butterfly's fluttering wings in the Sahara could alter a typhoon's course in the Pacific Ocean.

Science defines this energy as motion and this energy is in the form of the motion of molecules. The arrangement of molecules differs as the form varies. For instance, the energy making up your liver tissue is different from that of the heart, stomach, spleen, thyroid, pancreas, pituitary gland or any other tissue of the body. Also, the energy that makes up the pages of this book is obviously different than the energy that makes you.

The atoms that make up your body act like radio antennas broadcasting waves. Every person sends out different wave lengths. Your own personal wave lengths are just like your fingerprints. They are unique and different from everybody else. Each person and each individual part of the body produces different frequencies. This is why you can only accept an organ transplant from someone who resonates on a similar frequency. If you try to transplant an organ that resonates differently than the person who is accepting it, the organ will fail. Similar things happen with relationships. If both people are not on the same wavelength, they will not be compatible no matter how much they try to force the relationship. It always will end in heartache.

Researchers are now finding that this energy can become unbalanced and blocked because of trauma, stress, negative thinking, nutritional deficiencies, nervous system malfunction, etc. These imbalances create energy malfunction and may manifest themselves as mental disorders, disease, discomfort, etc.

Our bodies are constantly creating and sending out energy and taking in energy from the environment. Disease and disorder may also be caused by interferences in the natural vibrational frequencies. The primary objective may be the removal of these interferences to correct the overall balance in the body.

Therefore, to achieve and maintain health and wellness you must protect the energy flow throughout your body. This energy must remain unblocked and in constant balance.

Let me explain. Energy is always around us. It cannot be created or destroyed. It only changes. It just "IS". This is a Universal Law. Energy is a vibration or frequency that depends on what level it's resonating. How can we prove there is energy right now in your room as you read this book? Very simply—just bring in an AM/FM/satellite tuner and you will be able to pick up the music if you dial in the right frequency or resonation.

Here's an example of how this works in nature. An established tree drops a seed to the ground. A bird comes along and eats the seed. The bird gets as much nutritional value from the seed as it can and then excretes his waste on to the ground. The seed is now surrounded by its own fertilizer (bird feces) and sinks into the ground. If the environmental factors are suitable to the genetic makeup of the seed, then it will germinate and start to grow. As the tree grows it provides nutrients (via its leaves or fruit) and benefits all who take advantage of its resources (branches, leaves, shade etc.).

The inevitable will happen and eventually the tree will "die" —but not its energy. The energy just gets transformed. If it falls down and decays, the decaying tree will provide nutrients to the surrounding soil. It could also be cut down and used to fuel industry or heat our homes. Whatever is left that wasn't converted to energy will be absorbed back to the soil where it will fertilize the ground and provide nutrients for something else to take advantage of.

We too are made up of this energy. When we die, our energy goes somewhere beyond and what is left of our bodies will provide nutrients to the soil, or as some would say, "worm food."

As I mentioned before, this is how relationships work. Just as a vibration will resonate similarly to another vibration resonating at the same frequency, two people who are resonating at the same frequency on their first date will have dramatically greater chances for a second date. If it is not conductive, then it will not survive. How many times have you met someone and you didn't "click" no matter how hard you tried. If they are not resonating with you on the same frequency and in the right environment, then it will not work out. No matter how much you try to force it. The relationship will always end in heart break. It is like trying to plant a palm tree in Alaska. There may be fertile soil but the environment is not as conductive as it would be if planted near the equator. Maybe someday, with continental drift, Alaska's environment will be better suited for the palm tree—but not today.

Another example uses a baby grand piano and a crystal chandelier. You can strike one key at a time until you hit just the right key, with just the right frequency and that crystal will vibrate. Why? Because they are on the same frequency.

How many times have you heard or read the comment, "If you want to be successful you need to hang out with successful people." I once read that if you were to take your close friends and average their yearly salaries, the result would be about the same as your own salary. Have you ever wondered why this happens? Why does your environment play such an important role in whom you are and whom you become? To answer this you must go deep within your own mind and find the answer. It has to do with your conscious and subconscious mind.

Your conscious mind is your emotional mind. Your subconscious mind cannot pick and choose what to believe. Initially, from the time you were conceived until approximately four years old, the subconscious soaks up its environment like a sponge. After four, the conscious mind starts to develop and it assumes the role of "big brother" to your subconscious mind, monitoring anything that goes into it. The subconscious mind automatically supports what your conscious mind continually puts into it.

Your mind sees in pictures. How do I know this? Well, what if I were to say, "Don't think about your refrigerator." What just happened? If you own a refrigerator, and I am sure 99% of you do, you just saw a clear picture of your refrigerator in your mind.

I once attended a seminar where the speaker asked for a volunteer from the audience. The speaker instructed his volunteer to close his eyes and try to identify an object placed in his hand without looking at it. After a few seconds, the volunteer confidently identified a "pen cap."

The speaker then asked, "What color is the pen cap?" This he couldn't answer for sure because he was blindfolded. Let's explain what happened. Since most of us have held a pen cap in our hands, we have built synapses in our mind to recognize that particular object. Think about it. How many times in your life have you picked up a pen cap?

When the speaker asked about the color of the pen cap, the best the volunteer could do is offer a guess because his mind didn't have a clear picture. What usually happens in these circumstances is that the person holding the pen cap answers the question with whatever color of pen they themselves use most often. For example, many teachers would answer red because they correct papers with a red pen. People who work in the business world would probably pick the color black.

In order for me to help you set a solid foundation for your children, it is vital that we first paint a clear picture of what is happening in your own mind so you can be as effective and clear as possible when you teach your children.

The following diagram was initially presented back in the 1930's by

Dr. Thurman Fleet, founder of the Concept-Therapy Institute and was elaborated on by Bob Proctor. I have updated it.

I want you to picture what a brain looks like. 99.9% of you are probably forming a crystal clear image of a big, wrinkly grey sponge. Even my four year old son, Jack, would know what it looks like. I can only imagine what would happen if we were walking down the street and he saw a brain from some poor mangled road kill on the side of the road. His initial reaction would be, "EWWWWW! Dad, look at the brain!"

What if I were to ask you what the mind looks like? Most of you probably have a confused look on your face right now. What does the mind look like? The picture you see above was initially designed to give a clear picture of the mind so people can relate to it. Remember, awareness is the first key to making a change.

Your body has five senses—sight, sound, taste, touch and smell. These senses interact with your environment 24 hours a day, 7 days a week, awake or sleeping. You are always consciously or subconsciously aware of your immediate environment.

On the top half of the head in the diagram is where your conscious mind is. Your conscious mind is your filter. It has an advisor or counselor called ego. The ego represents and advises the conscious mind and together they protect the subconscious mind from what are considered "potential threats" (more on ego later). The conscious mind and ego decide what "belief" you will store in your subconscious mind and there it will sit forever or until you decide you want to change it. No matter if the belief is positive or negative.

Before we go any further we must first define belief and how it is incorporated into our mind. Merriam-Webster Online Dictionary defines a belief as:

1. a state or habit of mind in which trust or confidence is placed in some person or thing
2. something believed; *especially* : a tenet or body of tenets held by a group
3. conviction of the truth of some statement or the reality of some being or phenomenon especially when based on examination of evidence.[1]

It also goes on to explain that a synonym for belief is *faith*.

Where do our beliefs come from? Our initial belief systems are instilled genetically by our parents. Genetic beliefs are the ones preprogrammed for survival. Take a tree for example. A tree is made up of genetic beliefs called cells and these cells are genetically expressed in different areas to make up different parts of the tree, such as roots, bark, fruit or leaves. The leaves on the tree are genetic beliefs that provide energy to the tree via a process called photosynthesis. The bark protects the tree from its environment. The roots have genetic beliefs programmed to collect water to nourish the tree and also to create a sturdy foundation for the tree to stand tall. The fruit has the tree's seeds inside while providing a vehicle for the seed to travel in. These are all preprogrammed in order to allow the tree to have a good chance of reproducing and therefore perpetuate the species.

Every species has these genetic beliefs instilled to survive their environment and preserve the species. Squirrels have great balance, bats can see in the dark because of sonar, spiders create webs, chameleons have skin that changes color enabling them to camouflage themselves to better blend into the surrounding environment and fish have fins and gills. Deer have very good hearing, sight and smell. Everything in nature has these certain genetic beliefs.

What if the predetermined beliefs programmed into animals and nature are not in step with the environment? The species will become extinct. It happened with the dinosaurs and it is happening right now with the melting of the polar ice caps and destruction of the rain forest. In our near future the polar bear among other species could become extinct.

Similarly, humans have genetic beliefs that make our heart circulate the blood throughout our bodies. Our lungs are made from genetic beliefs that enable us to inhale oxygen and exhale carbon dioxide as waste. The efficiency of these organs varies from one person to the next, but they help us adapt to our environment so we can reproduce and perpetuate our species just like Mother Nature intended. Our species has been phenomenal in adapting to the environment. This is why you see our species populating most of the earth (at least above sea level).

The other initial beliefs are instilled by our environment—our family and friends, even the sources we are unaware of like the news media, advertising and even people we see in the grocery store. Subconsciously we soak up our surroundings, unaware that we are getting programmed with other people's beliefs.

Let me give you an example of how much our environment can influence our belief systems. The other night I was in my bathroom performing the evening ritual of brushing and flossing my teeth before bed. Many of us have done this so many that times it has turned purely into a subconscious event, meaning sometimes we don't even remember doing it.

How many times have you gone to bed and asked yourself, "Did I brush my teeth?" On your way to work, have you ever started to panic thinking that you forgot to put deodorant on? With one quick lift of the arm and a quick sniff to the underarm you could confirm whether you did or did not.

On one particular night I had a "peeper." As I pulled the drawer open to take some floss out, Alex, my 1 ½ year old son at the time, was standing in the doorway watching and absorbing every move I made. He watched as I took the floss container, opened it, pulled out an arm's length of floss and with a quick snap of my wrist, severed the string. I then twisted the floss around each of my index fingers and continued to start the process of flossing my pearly whites.

As I was flossing my teeth, I glanced over toward him and noticed a look in his eyes. It was an intense but calm look. It was as if he were absorbing everything I was doing. I smiled at him and he returned the smile and let out a small chuckle and continued on his merry way.

Later in the evening, as we were all lying in bed watching TV, I noticed Alex going through the motions of flossing his teeth in air. He pulled the imaginary floss out and made the same action with the wrists as I did to cut sever the floss from the container. He then carefully wound the imaginary floss around his fingers and continued to floss his teeth, seesawing back in forth. Then it hit me. I thought to myself, "My God, what do we have here?" Our children are a direct reflection of their environment. Everything in their environment gets soaked up in their minds. There is no preconception of good or bad.

Let's do an exercise to prove we all have heard or have some limiting beliefs about money. Please fill in the blank.

We aren't made of _____.
It takes _____ to make money.
Money is the root of all _____.
Money doesn't grow on _____.
We aren't made of <u>MONEY</u>.
It takes <u>MONEY</u> to make money.
Money is the root of all <u>EVIL</u>.
Money doesn't grow on <u>TREES</u>.

Do you ever wonder why most people follow in their parent's footsteps when deciding who to vote for or how they worship? Why does this happen? It is because it was programmed into their minds through their environment when they were a child.

Let me give you an example of one of the limiting beliefs I once had about people who had lots of money. As a child, I used to watch the popular TV show *Gilligan's Island* every day. For those of you who are not familiar with the show here is the plot. A group of seven castaways—a rich married couple, movie star, professor, farm girl, the Skipper and Gilligan—try to survive after they are shipwrecked on a Pacific island after what was supposed to be a three hour boat tour. The billionaire couple, Mr. and Mrs. Howell, was depicted as snobbish, too good for everybody else and all they cared about was their money. One of the implied humorous points of the show was that Mr. Howell continually failed to realize that all of the Howells' money is essentially useless to them on the island. They also refused to do any work and considered the other castaways as peasants.

I watched this show every day or years, constantly getting bombarded with the limiting belief of how "rich people" were snobs and thought they were better than everybody else. Are you starting to realize how we are programmed to think and act towards not only money, but with everything in our lives? These are all beliefs programmed into your subconscious mind by your environment. This programming starts even before we are born and still in our mother's womb. Even though we are safely tucked away within the confines of the womb we still pick up the external stimuli and vibrations of our mother's environment.

24 hours a day, seven days a week, the mind is constantly exposed to an assault from its immediate environment—ranging from our family and friends to TV and the internet. It is an assault from all sides and it doesn't stop. If you don't believe me watch an alcohol commercial or look at magazine advertisements. Do you ever see the negative effects of alcohol in advertisements? No, if they showed the heartache, car crashes and lives ruined from *irresponsible* drinking they would lose money, if not go bankrupt (I need to make a point here before I go on. I am not in favor of prohibition. I believe drinking is fine when you do it responsibly and in moderation). If they showed the aftermath of a car crash, where a drunk driver killed a two year old

child and ruined a family, do you think people would say, "It's beer drinking time!"?

What do you see in these advertisements? Open up a magazine or watch a commercial and I guarantee you will see an ad with beautiful women and men having a great time or some funny skit to get you laughing. Why do they advertise this way? They are trying to activate the pleasure parts of your brain to condition your mind to associate their brand of alcohol with what will give you pleasure. In 2006, according to TNS Media Intelligence, Anheuser-Busch spent $509.2 million on media advertising.

Big Pharma does the same with advertising their drugs. They are marketing geniuses. How else can you sell something with the possible side effects of rectal bleeding, stroke, suicidal thoughts or even death and still people will take it! The old adage that says, if you tell a lie long enough people will start to believe it is true. How about a lie with $509.2 million attached to it!

As a parent, you now are starting to become aware of how important it is to be careful about what you say, do and act around your children regarding money, relationships, addictions, work ethic, how to drive, deal with stress, etc. You are literally building in your children a belief system that will either limit them or allow them to excel in their future endeavors. If we are not constantly monitoring what we are doing, then we run the risk of unconsciously limiting our children, which can damage their ability to reach their fullest potential. More on how and why this happens in later chapters.

I know my wife and I want the very best for our children. We want to make sure we give them every opportunity to surpass us in every aspect of this beautiful journey we call life. All parents want this for their children. If we don't give them these opportunities then we fail as parents.

We have the huge responsibility to pass not only the belief of abundance, but how to instill the universal laws that govern our universe, so our children can prosper. They are in fact our future and this is what God wants us to do.

CALL TO ACTION EXERCISE

1. Allow your mind to welcome the abundance of God around you. Once you start realizing how much abundance is out there, you then can start the process of attracting it. This will allow you to enjoy this beautiful journey we call life and not allow the little things to bother you as much. Right now as I write these words, I am marveling at the infinite amount of newly fallen snowflakes outside my window. We have gotten over a foot of snow in the past 24 hours and I can only imagine how many snowflakes are out there. The number is infinite and would take more than a lifetime to count.

2. Stop watching the news and any other negative media. In time you may be able to watch it but not right now. In order for you to get the most out of this journey you must surround yourself with nothing but positive energy in all aspects of your life. When you don't watch the news for several weeks, you will find yourself feeling good and positive.

3. You must also start the process of cleaning up your children's environment. Monitor what your child watches on TV and the internet. Make sure their friends will have a positive impact on their life. You must do your best to make sure their environment is pure and positive.

Chapter Two

HOW THE MIND WORKS

The future depends on what we do in the present.
— **Gandhi**

H ere's how the mind works. Let's instill a new belief using, "I'm so happy and grateful now that I'm in the best shape of my life," as an example.

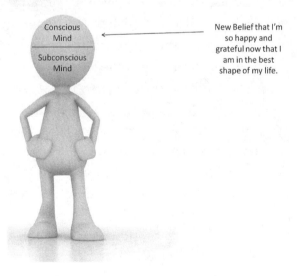

Conscious
Mind

Subconscious
Mind

New Belief that I'm
so happy and
grateful now that I
am in the best
shape of my life.

At this time your conscious mind has a choice to make—either discard the new belief as false, accept it as a new belief or put it in what I call "The Fog" of the mind. This is where you put beliefs that you are undecided about.

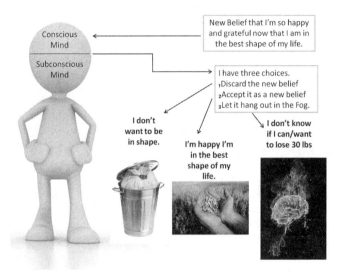

Discarding the new belief is easily identified. You just throw it right into the trash can. For example, assume that you have been a diehard political conservative your whole life. Everybody in your family is conservative. It goes back generations. Your great, great, great grandfather actually started the Republican Party.

If I came up to you and told you that you should be liberal how would you react? Well, after a few choice words you would probably start to laugh at me—even if I had all the concrete evidence in the world on why conservatism is evil and will lead to the downfall of our society. You would not instill this new belief. That is how deep rooted some of our beliefs are.

Some people's beliefs will never change because their ego has been protecting them their whole lives and it will resist change at all costs.

Accepting a new belief is also easily identified. I could tell you that there is an invisible force called gravity. If you don't believe me I can prove it by pushing you off a cliff. If you survive the impact you will have a newly established belief system concerning gravity.

"The Fog" of the mind is where the unidentified belief hangs out until you make your decision. It would be as if you were sitting at a train station, looking at a train track going in two different directions. You can't make a decision on which way to go, so you sit and wait while pondering which direction you should take. Have you ever wanted to start your own business or achieve a goal, but you don't take the steps to do so because of fear or the negative opinions of others? This is "The Fog" of your mind. Some people stay in this state of indecision their whole life. This is where procrastination comes in. Many times we want to instill change but procrastination sets in and puts out that internal fire for change. Sometimes this state of procrastination will last a lifetime.

You can come out of "The Fog" by taking your own conclusion about the belief. You can decide to kick the belief to the curb or accept it and store it in your subconscious mind.

All of our programmed beliefs are instilled from our environment: family, media, friends, etc. and some are hidden deep within our subconscious mind. Some of the limiting beliefs tucked back in our subconscious hold us back from success without our even realizing it.

The first step to changing your limiting beliefs is identifying them. How do you identify a limiting belief? You identify it by asking questions.

Let me share with you the story of one of my own limiting beliefs regarding money. When I was very young, my family lived in a trailer park for nine years. My mom and dad eloped when they were both teenagers. It was the middle of a blizzard and they ran away to Kentucky and got married in the aisle of an A & P grocery store. Just like many newlyweds, they had to struggle. After my brother and I were born, we all moved north, from Cincinnati, Ohio to Coldwater, Michigan. For the next decade we basically lived off the land. My dad hunted and fished for most of our food. He was in the beginning of his military career, so money was tight. I remember always being surrounded with the stress of not having enough money to pay the bills and afford the bare essentials. Don't get me wrong, my mom and dad provided a great life for my brother and me but there wasn't an abundance of money. However, there was an abundance of love.

When my dad moved up in rank in the military we moved to a very prestigious and wealthy town. My parents could not afford to buy a home in the area, so we rented a very small house. When I would invite "friends" over they would see how I lived and immediately labeled me as an outcast because my family was very poor. Every day I was tormented about the clothes that I wore and where my family lived.

As I grew older, finished college and entered into the real world I had no idea that I had a very limited belief system about money instilled in my subconscious mind from the environment when I was younger.

When I started my career as a Doctor of Chiropractic, I carried this limiting belief about money on my back like it was a bag of bricks without even realizing it. Whenever I had to tell one of my patients how much their care was going to cost I would start to feel uneasy and have butterflies in my stomach. Then, a feeling of guilt would surface because I had the subconscious belief that there wasn't an abundance of money and I would be taking away my patient's ability to buy food and provide for their family. What do you think my limiting belief was about asking for money or money in general? See the diagram below.

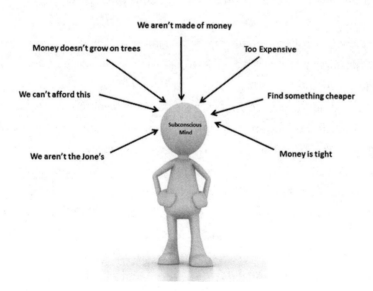

I started to ask myself questions. Why do I feel this way about money? Why do I think they cannot afford it? Why do I feel guilty about money?

The answer didn't come right away. It didn't come the next day or the next week. Three months went by and as I was driving in my car the answer suddenly popped into my conscious mind. I had subconscious limiting beliefs about money instilled into me by my environment when I was young.

I started to immediately analyze my own mind to see how much "limiting garbage" was clouding me from attracting more money. I also wanted to know how and why it appeared in my mind. I soon realized that not only was my environment "poor" when I was growing up but I also witnessed time and time again a poverty stricken mindset regarding money.

Whenever my father would have to pay for something he would always get upset. I remember comments he would make when he had to pay a mechanic to fix his car or to buy clothes, food etc. Whenever he had to pay for anything he always felt negative about the situation.

When I look back I sometimes grin at the wrath he would lay down onto the unsuspecting college kid that was unfortunate enough to be working the cash register that day. Many times I would hear, "It costs how much? This is way too expensive."

I remember feeling a couple of different emotions during these encounters. One was embarrassment for the confrontation and the other was fear that we really didn't have any money.

As these limiting beliefs repeatedly continued to show up in my environment, my mind solidified a limiting belief about money and it stored that limiting belief into my subconscious mind. Without even realizing it, I had a limiting belief that everyone around me didn't have enough money to pay for the necessities, let alone for the Chiropractic care I was providing. I carried this baggage around for years and I was living a very limited life.

Not only are many of us carrying around the limiting beliefs about money that we absorbed when we were younger but also about how we view the world and relationships, raising children, eating or dealing with adversity or different religious and political views, etc. The list goes on and on.

How you think and act in every situation is usually a direct reflection of your environment as a child. Some of the beliefs instilled by our environment can be very limiting and prevent you from reaching your fullest potential. Until you have identified these limiting beliefs you will continue to roam around in "The Fog" of life.

Are you starting to realize how important it is to monitor ourselves constantly on how we handle situations regarding relationships, money, work, eating, etc. We may not only be subconsciously limiting ourselves but also our children.

The first step to finding out if you have any limiting beliefs (and I'm sure you do) is to be aware of how you react and think in certain situations. Ask yourself why you react to these situations in a limited way. An easy exercise would be to analyze your thoughts the next time you feel upset, anxious, frustrated or stressed. Most people always point the finger at somebody else when they feel these emotions. Always remember, when you point the finger at something else there are three fingers pointing right back at you.

When you start to analyze yourself and question why you respond the way you do in particular situations the answer may not be immediately obvious. It may take days, weeks, months or even years. Once you identify a limiting belief, you must next start the process of replacing it with a positive belief.

Let me share with you another limiting belief I had about race. As I said, I grew up in a very small country town in eastern Michigan.

It wasn't a racist town but there just weren't any African Americans going to school with me. Every year we would travel to Cincinnati, Ohio to visit my relatives. On one particular visit, I was with one of my relatives in his car when someone cut him off. His response was, "Stupid nigger."

I was ten at the time and had never heard that particular term before. I remember when we went back home to Michigan I asked my parents what it meant. As you can guess, they were mortified. They sat me down and explained to me that the word was a bad word and it had no place in our family. I was satisfied with the answer and I put the word into the archives of my mind knowing if I ever said it I would be severely punished. However, the hatred that was displayed on my relative's face was the image that stuck. The emotional synapse that was etched into my mind was that people of color did selfish things like cut you off.

As I grew older, I was not aware I was subconsciously being programmed on the subject of African American culture by listening to negative rap music and watching movies like *Boys in the Hood* and *New Jack City*, which are very negative depictions of the African American race. Along with the negative media, my limiting belief on African Americans would be fueled by negative remarks I'd hear from small minded ignorant people in my community from time to time, like African Americans are drug dealing, gang banging thieves who take all the white peoples jobs. At the time, my conscious mind really didn't pay much attention to the comments because people of darker skin didn't directly affect my immediate environment. However, I was unaware that the comments were establishing their roots in my subconscious mind. Unbeknownst to me, I was in for a rude awakening in August 1996 when my racist belief about African Americans started to rear its ugly head as I checked into fall football camp at Western Michigan University (WMU).

As I was getting dressed for my first practice, I remember feeling uneasy not only because there were African Americans in the locker room, but my locker neighbor was a huge, tall, dark African American. I had a subconscious fear of this race. I remember feeling worried that I was going to get my possessions stolen. Then my imagination [fueled by ego's interpretation of past experiences] went wild and I started to fear for my life because of all the drive by shootings that were going to take place at practice. My ego, worried about its own self-preservation started to yell at me, "Are you nuts, you've seen *Boys in the Hood*, we gotta get out of here. You are going to die white boy. You need to go back home and do something else with your life."

Several weeks into the season, I found myself having some deep philosophical conversations about race with this African American teammate, Mario (who later became one of my closest lifelong friends). He would always listen to my questions and answer them, no matter how ignorant they were. I remember approaching him one day and saying, "What's up boy?"

He looked at me with anger and replied, "Don't ever call me boy."

"Why boy?" was my confused response.

Thank God Mario was patient with me. He sighed and went on to explain that the word wasn't bad, only if it was used with a bad intent. He perceived that I was using the word with the intent to condescend or belittle him.

I reassured him this was not the case. Over the years, after going to battle and sharing blood sweat and tears with all my teammates, I built a new solid belief system in my mind that everybody bleeds red regardless of the color of their skin.

I sometimes look back and laugh at myself and my old limiting beliefs but I am also saddened when I think of how many people go through life allowing their limiting beliefs to control them. I thank God for all the great positive experiences I received from playing football at WMU. Without it, who knows what kind of subconscious garbage would still be in my head and what kind of limiting belief systems I would be subconsciously passing down to my own children.

Once you have determined you have a limiting belief, you must immediately work on changing it or you will allow it to continue to hold you back. In the next chapter we will explain the process of achieving this.

CALL TO ACTION EXERCISE

1. Start identifying any limiting beliefs you have about everything in your life whether it is race, money, relationships, work, etc. Write them down because in the next chapter I will teach you how to change them and instill new positive belief systems.

2. Start analyzing your children for limiting beliefs. Start monitoring their environment for any limiting things such as negative TV, negative video games, etc. When you observe them acting out when they don't get their way, start asking yourself the question, "Where did they learn this?" Was it me, the babysitter, other family members, other kids, etc? Then, you can start the process of cleaning up their limiting environment.

Chapter Three

HOW TO CHANGE
A LIMITING BELIEF

A lot of people get impatient with the pace of change.
— **James Levine**

You have now started to think and analyze yourself. Like most of us, you are probably realizing how much subconscious baggage has been clouding your mind and limiting you in every aspect of your life.

We have achieved the first step, which is awareness of the limiting beliefs. We now have to replace the limiting belief with a positive one. We do this through the process called *conditioning*. We are going to start the process of conditioning your mind for success.

When I identified one of my limiting beliefs about money I immediately started to reprogram my mind through conditioning by using positive affirmations. "I'm so happy and grateful now that money comes easily to me. I'm so happy and grateful now that whatever I put my mind to, I can achieve. I'm so happy and grateful money comes to me in increased quantities from multiple sources on a continued basis," etc.

Let's look at the process with my new belief that *money is abundant*.

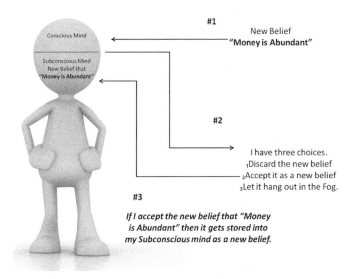

That was easy right? All I have to do is tell myself "money is abundant" and *POOF*, my belief will come into fruition—just like Aladdin's Lamp!

We need to stop here and analyze what happened when the movie, *The Secret* was released. *The Secret* was an outstanding movie and book about the *Universal Law of Attraction*. After watching the movie, many people thought that all they had to do was focus on what they wanted most and *poof* the magic genie would put a Ferrari [or whatever else they wished for] in their garage.

The Law of Attraction is one of many laws you must utilize in order for you to attract what you desire most in your life. The time it takes for true desires to turn into reality varies from person to person depending on how much garbage (limiting beliefs) is in the subconscious mind.

For example, how many people do you know, read or hear about that can attract success immediately? Then again, there are others who never seem to get out of their rut no matter how hard they try.

Let me explain how this process works using the *cola metaphor*.

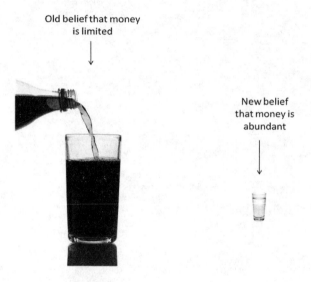

Old belief that money is limited

New belief that money is abundant

The picture above shows a small glass of water and large glass of cola. You will notice how the glass of cola is very large compared to the glass of water. Remember the example I used depicting how I grew up with a poverty mindset and the *Gilligan's Island* example depicting rich people as snobbish? You are constantly programmed and bombarded with beliefs on everything from your environment. So, over the years your environment has poured these negative and self-limiting beliefs into your mind. In my particular case, I believed that money was limited.

Many of us have limiting beliefs about money. We are raised to think money doesn't grow on trees, you don't talk to other people about money, people with an abundance of money are looked upon as bad and if you have too much money or you didn't struggle to earn it, you don't deserve it.

When you try to pour a conflicting new belief [the water] into an old dominant belief [the cola] you will soon find out that it is going to take more than a small dose of that new belief [or small glass of water] to make a difference.

How do we change the consistency of our mind to a clearer new belief? By using what is called *auto suggestion* or *positive affirmations*.

An affirmation is a tool used to reposition your mind to start to believe and attract the new belief. Some affirmations I personally use are:

- I am so happy and grateful now that money comes to me in increased quantities from multiple sources on a continued basis.
- I am so happy and grateful now that I keep a portion of everything I earn.
- I am so happy and grateful now that financial resources are lining up for me now.
- I am so happy and grateful now that I can feel my abundance growing daily.

As you say these affirmations you will pour more and more glasses of water into your cola filled mind and slowly you will start seeing a change. How fast or slow depends on how big your limiting belief cola glass is.

Let's turn our glasses of water to ice cubes, so you can get a clear picture in your mind. (Because our mind sees in pictures, correct?)

The more affirmations we say, the clearer the cola will get and our new belief system will start to take root into our mind.

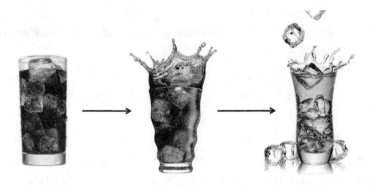

Let's take the limited belief of, "Money is the root of all evil." Since we have this huge tall glass of cola we must start the process of throwing ice cubes into our mind by using the affirmations of;

- I'm so happy and grateful now that money is good.
- I'm so happy and grateful now that money comes to me in increased quantities from a multitude of sources on a continued basis.
- I'm so happy and grateful now that God wants me to be prosperous and experience the abundance of this universe and through His strength anything is possible.

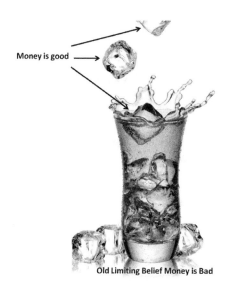

Money is good

Old Limiting Belief Money is Bad

Make as many affirmations as you desire but you must stay committed and say them every day, throughout the day. How long it takes to establish a new belief system depends on how deeply rooted the belief is. It may take minutes or years depending on how large your glass of cola is. Have fun with it.

This next step is critical. You must surround yourself with people who will support you in any goal or dream you want to accomplish. If not, you will allow your environment (your friends, family, negative media) to start pouring cola back into your mind and your progress will stall, or even worse, you may fall back into the unconstructive behaviors and attitudes that are far less than you deserve. The diagram below explains what happens when you do not surround yourself with people who support the new you. It is called *Crab Mentality* and I will expand on this in later chapters.

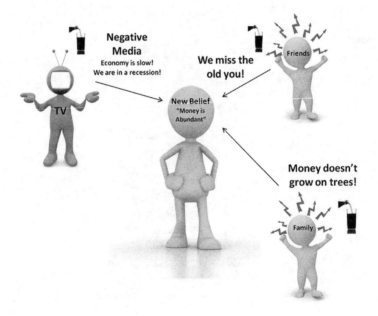

How many times have you tried to institute change in your life only to find that you get resistance from everyone in your environment? This happened to a client who I was coaching to improve her low self-esteem. Her entire life, she was told by friends and family that she was stupid and wasn't going to amount to anything. Let's analyze her mindset.

This garbage was engrained into her psyche throughout her childhood and teenage years. As soon as she decided it was time for her to change, she got resistance from everybody in her environment. This is why it is so important to make sure your environment is as pure as it possibly can be when you decide to institute change. If you do not get away from these negative comments you will find yourself falling into the old limiting beliefs that are far less than what you deserve.

You must stay committed to this new belief system no matter what happens. No matter if it rains on your parade, if somebody breaks up with you or you find yourself in a rut. Keep pushing forward. Rocky Balboa said, "It's not how hard you get hit. It's how hard can you get hit and keep moving forward. How much can you take and keep moving forward. That is how winning is done."

When you finally make a stand and refuse to back away from this "new you" your friends and family will have two choices. Accept the new you and resonate high with you or slowly fall to the wayside. The choice is theirs, not YOURS!

Usually they accept the new and improved you. Sometimes you even institute positive changes in their lives from your example and you can grow together on this journey.

CALL TO ACTION EXERCISE

1. You should have a list of limiting belief systems written down from the last exercise. Now, start the process of rewriting them so they are positive affirmations. For example, if you have a limiting belief system on money your affirmation could be, "I'm so happy and grateful now that money comes to me in increased quantities from multiple sources on a continued basis." If you have low self-esteem, then introduce positive affirmations about yourself like, "I'm so happy and grateful now that I am beautiful/smart/successful, etc." You can now start the process of dumping clear water into your old limiting cola belief. Repeat these affirmations throughout the day. Write them down and post them on your bathroom wall. Keep them in your pocket and say them out loud every chance you get. Repetition is needed here. Don't quit. Remember, the time it takes for a new belief system to build a synapse in your mind depends on how large your glass of cola is. Persist until you see a change and then persist even more.

Chapter Four

WORKING WITH THE UNIVERSAL LAWS

---

*"Winning is not a sometime thing, it is an all the time thing.
You don't do things right once in a while...you do them right
all the time."*
—Vince Lombardi

B ob Proctor explains in his seminar "A Lawful Process for the Creation of Wealth", which is based on Wallace D. Wattles book "The Science of Getting Rich", the seven natural laws of the Universe. They are as follows;

- The Law of Vibration
- The Law of Perpetual Transmutation (Law of Attraction)
- The Law of Gender
- The Law of Relativity
- The Law of Polarity
- The Law of Rhythm
- The Law of Cause and Effect

Unfortunately, you must utilize all the universal laws and not just one or two of them. What I am going to do is explain each one so you will have a clear picture in your mind in order to utilize them for yourself and your family.

The *Law of Vibration* states that everything in the universe is constantly vibrating. The universe is in a constant state of motion. If you were to look at the page you are reading under a very powerful microscope, you would see millions of molecules vibrating at a certain frequency to make up the matter that we call paper. Take a look around right now and marvel in the fact that everything in your environment is vibrating at a certain frequency to make up the specific objects we call a desk, couch, walls, bricks, pencils, pens, metal, even you!

Everything in the universe is in a constant state of motion. Have you ever walked into a room and picked up a negative feeling, or a "gut feeling" that something is out of place. God speaks to us through the Law of Vibration and when you have these feelings you must follow them. It's just like "Mothers Intuition." Moms know when there is something out of place.

One day, when I was a child my mom and I were sitting at home watching TV and she shot up off the couch and told me to get my shoes on because we were leaving. We jumped into the car and I asked her what was going on. She explained that she had a horrible feeling about my brother. An hour earlier, my brother had gone out with a group of friends who were up to no good. They were going to steal some candy from the convenience store and, unbeknownst to my brother, they were going to use him as bait to distract the unsuspecting cashier. We arrived just in time as they were about to go into the store. My mom jumped out and dragged my brother to the car and took us all home. We didn't find out until later that all the kids were caught and got into big trouble.

Later, after coming to the conclusion that my mom was "Wonder Woman" with super hero powers, I asked her how she knew something bad was going to happen. She just looked at me and smiled and said, "Mother's intuition, honey."

Becoming consciously aware of this vibration can also be called "feelings". The great thing about feelings is we can learn how to control how we feel in certain situations. That is, whenever you feel bad you can consciously choose to feel good. When you meet someone for the first time and you get a bad feeling about the person, you should follow what God is trying to tell you and stay away. We all have this ability to recognize and follow this gut instinct but many of us decide not to. This is God trying to talk to you through the vibrations of the universe and you should follow it every single time. You should never allow someone else's negativity to bring you down to their level. You always have a choice. This is why when you want to administer change in your life you always want to surround yourself with people who will help you on the journey, not hold you back.

Have you ever known people who actually talk themselves into getting sick? They will go around and say, "This time of year I always get a cold." A few days later they come down with the sniffles. You can make yourself sick or heal yourself through consistent thoughts. How many times have you heard of people praying for somebody who was on their deathbed and lo and behold they end up recovering.

I remember reading a story in 2010 about an Australian couple whose baby boy was prematurely delivered in a Sydney hospital after just 27 weeks gestation. Doctors came into the room and told the parents their son was dead. He then was given to his mother, who gently unwrapped his blankets and placed him on her chest so she and her husband David could say their goodbyes.

But after two hours of cuddles and being spoken to by Kate and David, baby Jamie began to gasp. Doctors said this was a 'reflex' but he began gasping more often and then opened his eyes. He ended up surviving and now is a healthy boy.

We all have this ability and can utilize it by consistently controlling our thoughts in a positive manner. This in itself will enable us to stay in a high resonation or vibration as previously discussed. Your thoughts are energy that go out into the universe and penetrate all time and space. Quantum Physics has proven this.

The *Law of Perpetual Transmutation,* also known as *The Law of Attraction*, is the transformation of non-physical (thoughts) into ideas, which stirs emotion, and allows you to take the necessary action steps toward manifesting anything you want to produce into the physical form. It is the ongoing change that never stops. God's universe as a whole is an ocean of motion. This motion is the only thing that is constant. Motion does not change but the energy of the universe does.

This energy is in a constant state of transmission (motion) and transmutation (change). Remember my explanation of what happens to a seed after a bird poops the seed on the ground. If the environment is resonating with the seed it will start to grow and eventually turn into a large impressive tree. This law explains that process. Everything is always moving and energy is always changing. It cannot be created or destroyed. It moves and changes form. This is how prayer works. When you pray, you stir up emotion and this movement between spirit and form allows you to speak the language of God and manifest itself into what you are praying for into form or your reality.

Let me give you an example. A client of mine was having a hard time with his business. He and his wife were in debt and living paycheck to paycheck. He was stressed and so was his wife. I was guiding and teaching him at the time about the mind and how this law works. He absorbed everything I taught him and applied it immediately. All day long he would pray to God by saying, "I'm so happy and grateful now that God has blessed me with money that comes to me in increased quantities from multiple sources on a continued basis." He would say this prayer/affirmation upon waking in the morning, throughout the day and it would be the last thing he said before falling asleep. He literally said this affirmation hundreds of times throughout the day. One month went by, then another, then three months passed and there was no increased money from multiple sources on a continued basis. To make matters more challenging, a huge lightning bolt struck his building and ruined all of the equipment on which he relied to operate most of his business. As I was speaking to him over the phone, listening to his sobs, I remember thinking to myself, "Holy cow, when it rains it pours."

I explained to him that he must remain positive about the situation. His focus was his reality, so it was crucial to consistently think positive thoughts because this is what he will attract. He must continue to push forward no matter what happens. His reply to these comments was a barrage of swear words directed at the frustrating situation he was in. I insisted he look at the positives of his life and not dwell on the negatives.

His reply was, "What positives? I'm in debt up to my eyeballs. My building is glowing from the recent lightning strike, which by the way fried $15,000 worth of equipment, and I have no way to support my family. How can this possibly get any worse?"

I explained to him that it could and will get worse unless he changed his attitude and started to look at the positives on what he perceived to be negative. He must stay in a positive resonation and be grateful for the things that he did have in his life, for example, the good health of his wife and two kids and how his business was right at the point of producing a positive cash flow. I went on to explain that even when we perceive events that happen in our lives to be negative, with time, we will see that they needed to happen in order for us to learn a lesson that would allow us to grow and prosper. He needed to learn this lesson or it would repeat itself. It is very easy to celebrate when you are on top but the real lessons are learned when you are at the bottom and have to deal with adversity. This is how character is formed. Life will continue to go up and down, but the trick is to not go down farther than you were before. You must continue to climb higher and higher. This is what God wants us to do. He wants us to grow in every aspect of our lives—spiritually, financially, mentally etc.

He took this new advice and continued to push forward and apply the universal laws which you are learning here. His business suddenly started to grow, even though he lost his equipment to the lightning strike. The month following the damaging storm was a record month and his business produced a very hefty profit. He called me to report the good news. I smiled and told him to continue on the path which got him there and to expect and desire more. If he did this, things would get even better. He just needed to continue on the path and apply what he had learned.

A month later he got a call from his insurance company and they were going to issue a check for $23,000 to replace all the equipment he had lost even though his original purchase price was only $15,000. Two days later the insurance company called again and, utilizing some type of formula, calculated the potential loss of income and issued him a check for an additional $25,000.

Let's stop right there and analyze what just happened. If he would have decided to have a pity party and stay in the negative resonation, do you think his business would have produced a record month? Probably not, but since he persisted and applied the same universal laws you are being taught here, his business grew to record levels. When the insurance company did their supplemental calculations to determine compensation for business lost, he was enjoying a record month so his reimbursement was very generous. If his business would have stayed where it was and not produced a record month, he only would have gotten a check from the insurance company for $1,500. He made a $23,500 profit for staying in a positive resonation. His focus became his reality. The biggest lesson he needed to learn was that his business wasn't even utilizing the very equipment he perceived at the time was essential to being profitable. He grew his business with his high resonating focus and that became his reality. Remember, people will always go where there is positive energy.

With the insurance check for the equipment he was able to upgrade everything and with his new found belief in himself and in his ability to persist, his company has continued to have record months and now record years. His wife has been able to stay at home and raise their two beautiful boys, which they both always desired. They live in their dream house in a very prestigious neighborhood. In his garage is the convertible he always imagined that he and his wife would go out to dinner in. He did all of this with his consistent positive thoughts/energy.

> *"Thoughts are sending out that magnetic
> signal that is drawing the parallel back to you."*
> **— Dr. Joe Vitale**

The *Law of Gender* states there is a gestation period for a seed to germinate into whatever it is supposed to grow into. You must be patient! We live in an instant gratification society. This is not how these laws work. If you have a goal to become multimillionaire and you live in a trailer, don't expect to see the millions of dollars showing up in your mailbox overnight. Everything takes time!

The universe does not care that you're impatient. It has been in existence over 12 billion years. Be patient and allow the laws to work for you and not against you. Everything will happen at the appropriate time.

The *Law of Relativity* is one of my favorites. All things are relative to one another and correspond with each other. All the Universal Laws are related to one another. Remember me explaining that you must utilize all the Universal Laws and not just pick a few. The Universal Laws must be in harmony with each other in order for you to get the most out of life. There is no poor or rich, slow or fast, small or big except when you compare the two. Let me explain. There is somebody out there better than you and there is somebody out there who you are better than. It is only when you compare yourself to one or the other that you can see the difference. It is confusing right? It really isn't. Refer to the figures below and you will see what I am talking about.

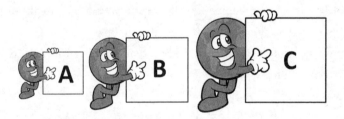

You can obviously see that box "B" is bigger than box "A". And box "C" is bigger than box "B". The truth is that Box "B" is neither big nor small. It just exists. We make box "B" whatever we want depending on how we use it.

One of the ways you can utilize this law is when you are trying to build your self-esteem. When you are comparing yourself to somebody else, don't compare yourself to a person who has already mastered what you are trying to achieve. This will only frustrate you and bring you down. Take for example the belts you see people wearing in Martial Arts. There are many different levels of belts. Usually, when you are a white belt it means you are a beginner. When you see a person wearing a black belt it usually means they have some sort of mastery of the technique. If you are in the middle wearing a brown belt you would rather compare yourself to a beginner than somebody who is a black belt. Doing so will allow you to feel better about yourself. Have fun with this law. Everything in your life is energy, it just exists.

The *Law of Polarity* states that everything in the universe has an equal and opposite—Ying and Yang. There is light and there is dark. There is front and back, right and left, up and down. Everything in this universe just exists. This law states that you have a choice when responding to any situation in your life. You can view it as being positive or negative. Again, remember the business owner with the lightning strike. He chose to look at everything as positive. Another example would be people who have survived a violent crime. How can somebody who has been raped respond to it differently than somebody else who experienced the exact situation? One decides to be a victim while the other decides not to. In one situation the person grows from the event and becomes a stronger, better person while the other will carry around the burden like a bag of bricks for the rest of their lives and allow the act to limit them in every aspect of their life. What it comes down to is this, "Do you see the world as a glass half full, or half empty?"

The *Law of Rhythm* states that to every action there is a reaction. The tide comes in and goes out. The sun rises from the east and sets in the west. The Earth and other planets in our solar system revolve around the sun. Everything is in a constant rhythm. You are going to have good days and bad days. These bad days allow you to enjoy the good days. Even when you are having a bad day, God has given you the ability to have what is called *free will*. We can choose to react to those days in a positive or negative way.

The *Law of Cause and Effect* states that every cause has an effect and every effect has a cause. Are you as confused as I was when I first read that? Basically, it states that nothing in the universe will ever happen unless it is governed by the Universal Laws. These laws are like gravity. You can tell me that gravity does not exist but if I push you off a roof you will become a believer. The same is true with the Universal Laws. You can utilize them to have the life of your dreams or you can allow them to continue beating you down. It is your decision. The laws do not care whether you utilize them or not. They just "are."

Now that you have been introduced to how the Universal Laws govern the universe, you must learn them in order for you to build positive belief systems within yourself and your children.

When you want to change a belief or instill a new one, you must experience emotion along with your thought to make an emotional connection to whatever you are trying to attract (Law of Vibration). There are only two types of emotions—positive and negative. When we combine either positive or negative emotions with a person, place or thing then we can experience an infinite amount of feelings like love, gratitude, compassion, happiness, anger, fear, sadness, guilt, etc.

If you do not have an emotional connection with your new belief then it turns into a wish. Merriam-Webster Online Dictionary defines a wish as:

To have a desire for (as something unattainable).

The old saying goes, "Poop in one hand and wish in the other and see what fills up first."

Wishes stay dormant until we fuel them with our emotions. Do you get it now?

Look at the diagram.

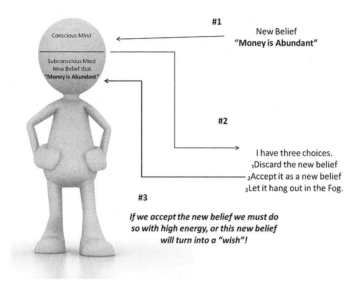

What happens next is truly remarkable.

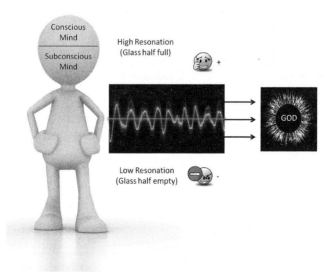

Here we have our mind model. The frequency band you see is resonation. Resonation (Law of Vibration) is an energy field you send out to God. This is your communication link to God. Remember when I said that whatever you focus on becomes your reality (The Law of Attraction)? God's abundance is all around you as well as innately inside you. It resonates through you as your talents, ideas and inspiration longing for you to express it. But you must be aware of it, figure out a way to harness it and be able to use it. Your powerful mind is the connecting link where all this magic takes place. Your consistent thoughts can turn into a belief and with the right attitude you may have the ability to directly speak and resonate with your divine power.

You have a choice on how to resonate at all times. You can resonate high with the emotions of love, compassion, joy, abundance, happiness, drive, enthusiasm, gratitude, passion, etc. Or, you can resonate low and experience the emotions of fear, guilt, anger, frustration, impatience, sadness etc.

God sits out in the universe accepting the energy you send to Him. Since He gave us the power of free will, He will give you whatever you resonate the most. That is, if you resonate positive then you will get positive. Resonate low and you will attract negative.

In my humble opinion you should always resonate high or "glass half full" (Law of Polarity). What emotions resonate high? All the positive emotions like love.

Now, let's see how it all works. Let's say we have a new established belief in our subconscious mind. For instance, "Money is Abundant". Attach the positive emotion of love to this new belief. When the belief "Money is Abundant" is tied together with the emotion of love, I will experience the feelings of gratitude, happiness, excitement etc.

See the diagram on the next page.

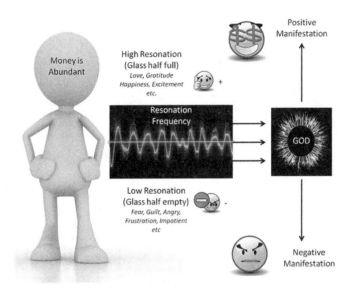

You must stay in the high resonation frequency if you want to attract your new goal and solidify your new belief system into your subconscious mind. If you choose to fall into a low resonation, you will not attract your new goal and it will shatter your new belief system. As a result, you will not attract God's abundance and you therefore will fall back into the old behaviors and attitudes that are far less than what you deserve.

God will provide you with whatever you want. He gave us the wonderful gift of free will. We get choose how we want to live this life. Matthew 7:9 NIV says, "Which of you, if his son asks for bread, will give him a stone?"[2] God will supply you with whatever you think and desire most, whether it is positive or negative.

Your mind is just like fertile soil. It will produce whatever seeds you plant in it. The fertile soil doesn't care what you plant. It's up to the individual to decide what they want to plant. For example, let's say you have two seeds. In one hand is the seed of corn, the other is a seed of poison ivy. You dig two holes and plant both seeds in the fertile soil.

Over the weeks you care for both seeds by watering, fertilizing and making sure they get plenty of sun.

What happens? The fertile ground will produce an abundance of poison ivy just as much as it will corn. It doesn't care if corn provides nourishment and poison ivy provides an irritant or even death if you are allergic.

The mind is more complicated and magnificent than fertile soil but it works the same way. Whatever kind of seeds you imprint onto the subconscious mind will determine what will grow into "your crop." Just like the Bible says, "As you sow, so shall you reap."

I know what you're thinking, "It can't be that easy." I know, I thought the same thing when I started on my journey, but you must understand that you have had blurry vision and have not seen clearly your whole life. When I was younger I thought everybody saw the world as I did. I passed every eye exam they gave at school, so according to my belief system I had "normal" eyesight, which meant everybody saw like I did. It wasn't until I was in 8th grade, at a high school basketball game, that I discovered the true reality of not everybody seeing the world as I did. I was sitting with a friend and he looked across the court and said, "Look across the basketball court. Jeff, Trevor and Paul are sitting over there."

I looked over and saw nothing but a blurry glob of people. I replied, "How can you see them, Curt?"

He handed me his glasses and said, "Try these."

When I put the glasses on a whole new world was opened up for me. This is how a belief system can instantly be changed in a matter of seconds. Before I put the glasses on I had an old belief that everybody saw the world like I did. Now, when I was offered Curt's glasses I could have let my ego rear up and say, "I don't need your stupid glasses, I see just fine," just like many people do when presented with a new idea or concept. I decided to take a chance and have a little faith. When I put those glasses on a whole new world of opportunity arose from the blurry shadows. Instantly my belief changed and I am sure my eyes were as big as saucers when I realized how clear the world could be.

This book serves as your "prescription glasses" enabling you to start to see life clearly and allow the miracles of the universe work for you and not against you. I didn't come up with these laws, God did. Have the faith to put on the glasses and marvel in the fact of how much clearer the world will be. It works!

We can't keep thinking about why certain perceived negatives happen in our life. I'm sure when we die God will replay the movie of our lives and explain why events had to happen in order for this cosmic dance to continue to work.

The other day on my way to the clinic, I got a call from my assistant, Dee, at 6:30 am. I knew something had to be wrong if she was calling this early. I answered and jokingly said, "Did our clinic burn down?"

She replied calmly, "Dr. Garrett, I think somebody just stole my car."

I told her to lock the door and I would be there in five minutes. When I got to my office I saw that, sure enough, Dee's car was gone. Actually, it was her daughter's car. Her husband's car had a problem with the alternator so he was using her car and Dee ended up borrowing a car belonging to her daughter who was out of town. Do you see how funny this cosmic dance is? All these events had to take place in order for *this* thief to steal *this* car.

When I walked inside Dee was sitting there with a smile on her face. I asked her why she was smiling and she told me that as she was preparing for the day she heard a honk and saw the car drive off. The car thief honked! I thought this was kind of funny. Who honks good bye as they are stealing somebody's car? We ended up getting a laugh out of the audacity of this comical thief.

Now, Dee had two choices on how to respond to this car theft. First, she could "freak out" and allow this situation to affect her whole week in a negative way (99% of society would probably make this choice). She could have moaned and groaned about how horrible her luck was, saying that bad things always happen to her. She could have had a pity party with the invitation reading, "Why me?" To most people, this event probably would have ruined their entire year.

Not Dee. We both laughed and joked about how this guy probably needed the car more than she did, especially when he gave her a honk to say thanks for the car. We will never know the reason why, on this particular day, her car was stolen. Perhaps her daughter would have gotten into an accident the following week or maybe this guy needed to be a particular place at a particular time for this cosmic dance to continue. The speculations are infinite. We will never know. But one thing is for sure, you can always choose how you feel when something happens in your life, even if the event would be perceived as negative by the majority of the population. Dee chose to perceive it as a positive so she resonated positive. When this happens you attract more positive.

CALL TO ACTION EXERCISE

1. Start the process of allowing the Universal Laws to work for you and not against you. Allow yourself to stay in a high resonation no matter what happens in your life.

2. Remember, challenges in life occur in order to teach us valuable lessons we must learn before we go further down the path. Look at every challenge in your life as a chance to grow and be excited when these challenges show up. If you learn from the challenges, growth will be coming your way in some aspect of your life. If you do not learn from these

challenges, then they will continue to resurface over and over again, limiting your life.

3. You must stay in the high resonation no matter what. You become what you consistently think about most. If you are having a bad day, you'd better turn it into a great one real quick or you will attract more bad. You can't afford to ever allow yourself to fall into this negative resonation. Remember, your kids will not always listen to you, but they will never fail to imitate you.

Chapter Five

EGO

Anytime there is a struggle between doing what is actually right and doing what seems right, then your ego is interfering with your decision.
—Darren L. Johnson

It has been said that a positive thought is 10,000 times more powerful than a negative thought. You want to always stay positive about any situation in your life. When you stay positive you resonate at a higher level. Don't ever let any negative thoughts come into your mind. If you let the negativity into your mind, it will take you longer to manifest whatever you are trying to attract.

NFL Pro Bowler, Jason Babin, a friend of mine, was giving an interview with Graham Couch of the Kalamazoo Gazette in December 2010 when he was asked about "doubting himself." His response was perfect.

"There's always that little bit of doubt, but as soon as you get that little bit of doubt, you've got to squash it, because if it's in

your mind, if it's how you think, how you view yourself, that's how you become. And I always viewed myself as a Pro Bowler, as a guy that could be the top of the league and a top performer in the NFL. I've always felt that way in my heart. I've prepared that way, I train that way, I live my life that way. Thankfully I've gotten the opportunity this past year to prove it to everybody else."
—Jason Babin

Easier said than done right? You will be tested by your environment. Your family, friends, colleagues and enemies (if you have any) will test your new found belief.

Approach these tests as a sign of growth. Any failure you experience is telling you that something bigger and better is on its way or you needed to go through that particular failure to learn a lesson before you go further down your path (just like my client with the lightning strike). You will keep getting the same lessons until you learn from them.

Keep pushing and taking action toward whatever you want to accomplish. Along your journey I guarantee you will experience good times and bad times (Law of Relativity). Do not let fear take control while you experience the bad times. You must stay in control of your life. Whenever you feel fear you must understand that this is your ego trying to hold you back. Fear is false evidence appearing real.

Let's explain how ego fits into this equation. First we must define ego. Ego is the definition of oneself built from your past and present experiences. It is a mediator between your conscious and subconscious mind. If you give it permission, your ego will volunteer itself to be the gatekeeper of your mind and decide what belief may exit and enter your subconscious mind. Ego is *advisor* to your conscious mind. If you want to grow to a higher level in any aspect of your life, you should always have your ego in check.

Since your ego is formed by the combination of your past and present experiences, it does not like and appreciate change. It must be treated like a child. As we all know, children must be taught and disciplined along the way in order for them to differentiate between right and wrong and become productive members of society. If you do not discipline your ego, it will run rampant and act like a two year old flailing, kicking and screaming when challenged.

MEET YOUR EGO

I DON'T WANT TO CHANGE!

How many people do you know who refuse to admit or apologize when they are wrong? When they are challenged they will revert back to what I call "Middle School Syndrome." "Middle School Syndrome" is when the egotistical maniac finds something that another person is sensitive about and teases him about it. This could be a variety of things ranging from something as trivial as appearance to something the person did in the past they are ashamed of. This is all the result of ego running amuck.

To me, ego is the devil. If you analyze your ego you will find that it holds you back from God's abundance. How does the ego do this? It resists your growth. How many times have you started something and not finished it because of an excuse. I wanted to lose 35 pounds but I didn't have time to diet. I wanted to quit my job and start my own business, but the economy is bad and I'm fearful I might fail. I wanted to ask the beautiful girl down the street on a date, but I'm afraid she won't like me. Yes, ego is the devil, so to speak. The ego is always trying to knock you off the path to God's abundance. The abundance you and your children deserve!

Again we will refer to the diagram.

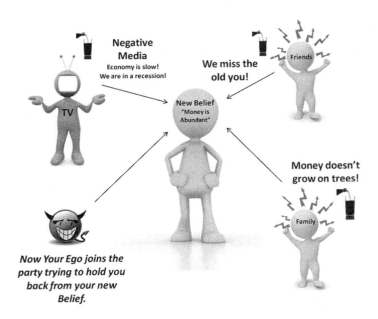

At times your ego will do everything in its power to hold you back. All sorts of challenges will surface that you never thought were even possible. As these challenges surface, if you sharpen your sword, stay positive, keep doing the affirmations and use the other tools you will learn in this book, you will overcome them.

The ego is what holds most people back from achieving a life of abundance. After applying the Universal Laws for a few days or weeks, if nothing happens they get frustrated (low resonating emotion). Ego is the pilot of your jet traveling to failure. You will hear your ego on the intercom saying, "This is your Captain speaking. Congratulations you failed again. I told you not to try to change. Now sit back and relax and enjoy the flight as I fly you to your destination called hell."

Most people will listen to this inner voice and go back to their old limiting thoughts, behaviors and actions. As soon as they revert back they will attract more of this negativity and failure. It is an out of control downward spiral to what I believe is living a life of hell. Ego is what destroys your friendships, marriages, relationships with your children and job performance.

You have to remember, God will provide you with whatever you want. He gave us the wonderful gift of free will. We get to make a choice about how we want to live this life. Remember what Matthew 7:9 NIV states, "Which of you, if his son asks for bread, will give him a stone?"[2]

God will supply you with whatever you think and desire most, positive or negative.

Look at the diagram. On the next page.

As you can see, your ego hangs out in the low resonation trying to hold you back from succeeding in your desired positive manifestation.

Dr. Joe Vitale, a motivational speaker said, *"If you turn it over to the universe you will be surprised and dazzled by what is delivered to you. This is where magic and miracles happen."*

Ego is why most relationships have problems. How many times have you argued with your significant other because of ego? You get

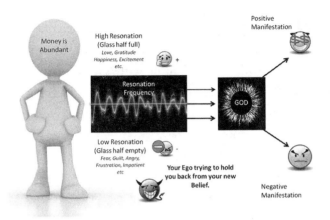

offended by what the other person did or didn't do or say. If you believe as I do that ego is the devil, do you think he wants your relationship to be filled with love or end in heartache? Most problems in any relationship are caused by lack of communication, resulting in one or both sides feeling as though they are not getting the love they deserve or the respect they need. Ego is like a shark that senses blood in the water and attacks viciously by clouding your head with comments like: He/She's disrespecting you. Don't give in. Keep being stubborn. Why should you say, "I'm sorry" when it is his/her fault that he/she is so insecure. He/she is not showing me any love. There is probably another person in their life. I'm sure he/she is cheating.

Sound familiar? Ego (devil) definitely plays a role in the destruction of many relationships if not monitored consistently. An apology goes along way doesn't it? When you apologize you bypass your ego and limit its power over you.

When I started my own personal journey, I realized I was holding a tremendous amount of guilt and sadness (low resonating feelings) in my mind because of the people I hurt in the past. I knew I had to let go of this baggage I was carrying around in order to start attracting the things I desired most. I immediately made a list of everybody I consciously knew I had hurt in the past and started the process of asking for their forgiveness. I utilized Facebook and other social media to get in contact with them. I can honestly say every person, except one, wrote back and accepted my apology. Here is the beautiful thing about forgiveness: once you ask for it, even if they don't accept the apology, it frees your mind. In Colossians 3:13 NIV it says, "Bear with each other and forgive whatever grievances you may have against one another. Forgive as the Lord forgave you."[3]

It is their burden if they don't forgive you. Once you ask for forgiveness you do not have to carry the cross on your back anymore. Jesus already did this for us. The next step is to also forgive yourself, which I know can be hard to do in some cases. I know this personally because I had to forgive myself for some things I had done in my past. A great technique for starting the process of forgiving yourself and for forgiving the people who hurt you in your past is to write the *Forgiveness Letter*.

Here is how the Forgiveness Letter works: Write [not type] down all of your feelings toward the person(s) about why they did this to you. Make sure you explain throughout the letter how it made you feel. After you have spilled your guts, whether it is a paragraph or 20 pages, you close the letter with, "I'm so happy and grateful now that I forgive you and we are now at peace." Then sign your name.

DO NOT MAIL THE LETTER! Take the letter somewhere safe and burn it. When you light the letter on fire watch, hear and smell it burn. This action signals to your mind that you are releasing the burden. That was easy, wasn't it? Now, do it for the next 30 days straight. If you miss a day you must start over. When I did this exercise I was pouring out all of my emotions in the beginning and by the end, because it didn't bother me anymore, my letters were only a few sentences long. Just like everything else with the mind you must use repetition to get a result.

When you need to forgive yourself for past actions then simply write a letter to yourself pouring out your feelings of disapproval for what you have done and what you have failed to do. You can end your letter with the affirmation, "I'm so happy and grateful now that I have forgiven myself and I am at peace with the world". Then just like before, light it on fire and watch, hear and smell it burn for 30 days straight. If you find yourself still feeling guilty at the end of the 30 days, start over and do it again for another 30 days.

Asking forgiveness and settling the wrongs you have committed in your life is like spring cleaning for your mind. Let me share with you another spring cleaning event I had to do to release the negative emotion of guilt from my closet. When I was in high school I was at a friend's house. He lived out in the country and had quads (four wheelers). On this particular day, another one of our friends, who was not present, had left his quad there so he wouldn't have to constantly bring it over in his truck. The other two guys there had their own quads and they said, "Andy wouldn't mind if you drove his."

I jumped on board and we went riding. We were having a great time jumping hills and tearing up the trails until I was climbing a really steep hill. Now, for those of you who haven't ridden quads, when you go up a steep hill you want to downshift in a lower gear, so you will have the power to make it up the hill. Long story short, I shifted up to a higher gear, which stopped the quad and it started to roll backward. I jumped off and watched in horror as it tumbled down the hill completely bending the frame. It still ran, but it was really beat up and I felt horrible. We called Andy and he came over to see the damage. I apologized several times. He told me not to worry about it, but you could see it hurt him to see his quad all bent up. I was 16 years old at the time and there was no way I could afford to pay for the damage I had done. I still offered, but he declined being the great person he is, but I still should have paid for the repairs.

Recently I noticed I was still feeling guilty about something I had done in the past. I searched my thoughts and this event popped into my mind. I felt guilty for not only taking his quad out without his permission but not owning up to my obligation to pay for the damage. I immediately contacted him on Facebook and asked for his address. I sent him a $1,000 check explaining I was fulfilling an obligation I had failed at in the past. Below is the letter I sent.

Dear Andy,

There is a chapter in my book devoted to asking for forgiveness from people we have wronged in the past. It reads as follows:

When I started my own personal journey, I realized I was holding a tremendous amount of guilt and sadness (low resonating feelings) in my mind because of the people I hurt in the past. I knew I had to let go of this baggage I was carrying around in order to start attracting the things I desired most. I immediately made a list of everybody I consciously knew I had hurt in the past and started the process of asking for their forgiveness. I utilized Facebook and other social media to get in contact with them. I can honestly say every person, except one, wrote back and accepted my apology. Here is the beautiful thing about forgiveness: once you ask for it, even if they don't accept the apology it frees your mind. In Colossians 3:13 it says, "Bear with each other and forgive whatever grievances you may have against one another. Forgive as the Lord forgave you."

Asking forgiveness and settling the wrongs you have committed in your life is like spring cleaning for your mind. Let me share with you another spring cleaning event I had to do to release the negative emotion of guilt from my closet. When I was in high school I was at a friend's house. They lived out in the country and had quads (four wheelers). On this particular day, another one of our friends, who was not present, had left his quad there to ride so he wouldn't have to constantly bring it over in his truck. The other two guys that were there had their own quads and they said, "Andy wouldn't mind if you drove his."

I jumped on board and we went riding. We were having a great time jumping hills and tearing up the trails until I was climbing a really steep hill. Now, for those of you who haven't ridden quads, when you go up a steep hill you want to downshift in a lower gear, so you will have the power to make it up the hill. Long story short, I shifted up to a higher gear, which stopped the quad and it started to roll backward. I jumped off and watched in horror as it tumbled down the hill completely bending the frame. It still ran, but it was really beat up and I felt horrible. We called Andy and he came over to see the damage. I apologized several times. He told me not to worry about it, but you could see it hurt him to see his quad all bent up. I was 16 years old at the time and there was no way I could afford to pay for the damage I had done. I still offered, but he declined being the great person he is, but I still should have paid for the repairs.

This, my friend is why you see a check written out to you for $1,000. This is a debt that I must pay, so please accept it with open arms. I will end with one of my favorite quotes from Muhammad Ali. "Service to others is the rent you pay for your room here on earth."

With sincere love and gratitude,
Garrett Soldano

I firmly believe we must own up to everything we have done to have a clear conscience. Remember, if you hold negative emotions about anything you must instantly rectify them or suffer the negative consequences of attracting more negative things in your life. Remember the diagram.

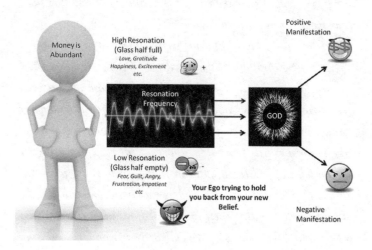

I had a client who was carrying around a tremendous amount of guilt for killing another person in a car crash. It wasn't his fault but he still couldn't let go the fact that he was involved in this person's death. Along with doing the 30 day forgiveness letter I also had him write a letter to the family of the person who was deceased. In the letter he explained how sad and sorry he was for their loss. He mailed the letter and several weeks later the wife called and reassured him she knew it was an accident and she didn't hold any animosity towards him. She also explained how thoughtful and meaningful the letter was to her and the family. She ended the conversation saying, "You must now quit carrying the baggage around your back and let it rest. My husband was a great man and this is what he would have wanted."

I couldn't have said it better myself. Holding on to guilt is like having roadblocks put up along your path preventing you from continuing your journey to the life of your dreams. Remove the roadblocks and continue down the path to your true destiny. If you continue on the right path, God's miracles will start to surface. Little ones at first, but they will eventually explode into an avalanche of abundance you could have never imagined. How well you practice the Universal Laws will determine the amount of time it will take for your goals to manifest (Law of Gender). You can apply these Universal Laws to any new belief that you desire, be it health, wealth, happiness, etc. The sky is the limit!

Right now, as you are reading these words you can instantly institute change in your life and that of your child. It just takes one thing—a thought. You must then follow that thought with the decision to get it done. Once you finally decide to accomplish what you truly want to do, taking persistent and consistent action everyday towards your desired thought will find you beginning to attract the very things you desire most in your life.

CALL TO ACTION EXERCISE

1. Whenever you feel your ego rearing its ugly head, stop, take a deep breath and ask yourself why you are feeling the way you do. You always have a choice when responding to somebody else's actions or words. Remember if you allow your ego to control your life you will live a very limited life. Sit the little devil down on a bench and let it cry like a spoiled two year old. Don't allow yourself to buy into any excuses that will limit your growth.

2. If you are carrying around any baggage from your past, now is the time to start the process of forgiveness. Utilize social media and other avenues to contact the people you have wronged and ask them for forgiveness.

3. Start doing the "Forgiveness Letters" for 30 days without missing a day. Make sure you complete the exercise and

BURN them. If you miss a day then have the discipline to start over. This proves to yourself and to God that you are really sorry for the acts you have done and failed to do.

Chapter Six

HOW TO PROGRAM
YOUR CHILD FOR
SUCCESS

"Children have never been good at listening to their elders, but they have never failed to imitate them."
—James Baldwin

Here is a diagram of your mind

Here is a child's mind from 0-4 years of age

As you can see in the illustration, the top half of the child's mind is absent. The conscious mind is still in development. A child's mind from 0-4 years old is like a giant soup bowl in which everything from their environment goes directly into the subconscious mind and serves to build a belief system about everything in life.

I was at the grocery store one day and met up with a friend of mine who has a beautiful three year old daughter. As we were talking, she started to jump up and down holding her private area. Her dad noticed this and asked, "Honey, do you need to go potty?"

"No daddy," was her reply. She continued to perform the "potty dance".

Again the dad asked her, "Are you sure you don't need to go potty?"

"No daddy," she replied again with a grimaced look on her face.

Exactly one second later the backside of her shorts exploded with poop. The poop was all over her back. Now, as parents, we have all experienced this scenario. There are not enough baby wipes in the world to clean up that mess. It seems that nothing short of bringing in a hazmat crew to clean up the nuclear explosion of poop will be adequate to take care of the mess. An ordinary washer/dryer cycle can't clean these clothes. You feel as if throwing them into a red bag that warns "Hazardous Material Inside" [with a big picture of a skull and crossbones] is the only appropriate course of action.

He had that look of, "What in the halibut do I do now?" He looked at her and said with frustration, "Honey, why didn't you go to the bathroom and go potty?"

She looked up at her father with the same frustrated look and with hands on her hips and head tilted to one side she replied, "I didn't have to go potty. I had to go poopy!"

Not only is this story hilarious [even more so because it wasn't my child], but it teaches us a valuable lesson in how a child's mind works. In her mind, potty meant going pee and poopy implied taking a poop.

There is no conscious reasoning just yet, only what she'd already soaked up from her environment during her very short life.

Kids soak up their environment. They are like a sponge. How many times have you heard your child react to something the same way you did? I know it's happened at my house. The other day, while I was working in the garage, something broke when I dropped it on the floor and I said, "Shit!" I looked up to find my son giving me a look like he had just discovered the theory enabling faster than light space travel. It seemed like he was shaking his head and thinking, "Yes, I have discovered how I'm supposed to react when I drop something."

Lo and behold, later that SAME day my little son Jack dropped his toy and guess what his reaction was? The familiar word, "Sit!" (He was still working on getting the letter "H" in there ☺)

I wouldn't have been surprised if he looked toward me after saying the universal word of frustration to give me a "thumbs up" with a look of accomplishment saying, "Don't worry dad, I've got this"!

I did, however, see the look of disapproval from my wife.

Everything in our children's environment from 0-4 years of age gets dumped directly into the subconscious mind building belief systems, positive or negative, that will directly inhibit or propel them throughout their life.

Their immediate environment builds belief systems and molds their minds to determine how they deal with relationships, money, eating habits, spirituality, political affiliations, stressful situations, driving, horrible addictions ranging from alcoholism to drug usage, procrastination…. Everything!

Do you now see how important it is to not only control your own mind and actions, but especially what is happening in your child's environment? If done the right way your child's belief system can look like the picture on the next page.

If programmed the right way, your child's belief systems can be pure and untouched. It is their environment that will dictate how much cola gets poured into them. Let's take a look at what happens to a child when his/her environment is not monitored the right way.

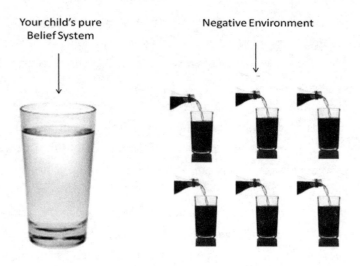

Or another way of looking at it would be the diagram below.

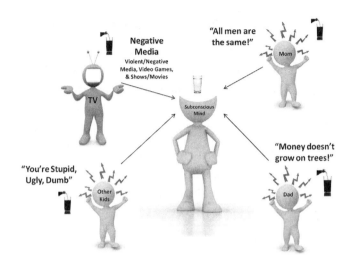

The other day my mom got my son, Jack, a McDonald's Happy Meal. The toy inside resembled Simon of *Alvin and the Chipmunks* (from the old cartoon, now a hit movie). Jack was so thrilled—you'd think he just discovered the Holy Grail!

We all know how grandparents love to spoil their grandchildren and I'm not a poster boy for the prohibition of fast food, but we all know if you eat fast food like cheeseburgers, fries chicken nuggets, pop etc. in excess it could be very unhealthy. As a responsible parent, I make sure that when they are on "my watch" I limit as much unhealthy food into their body as possible. I always ask people, "Would you put 87 octane gasoline in a Ferrari?" The answer is always no because if you want your sports car to perform at its best you must put in the best fuel you can. Our bodies are more amazing and magnificent then any car, but it works the same way. If you do not believe me, eat a dozen donuts an hour before running a mile. Keep track of how you feel during and after the run and write down the time it took you to run it. Several days later eat a grilled chicken salad an hour before and note how you feel during and after the run and write down your mile time. I'm sure you will definitely see and experience the difference between the two.

As Jack was carrying around his "Holy Grail" I started thinking about all those cool little toys I'd found in Happy Meals when I was a child. Then it hit me. How in the halibut can I remember most of the Happy Meal toys I received 20 years ago but I can't even remember what I got from my wife for Christmas 2 years ago?

Easy….they built a synapse in my mind by creating an emotional event, which I can recall at any given time. Like many corporations, McDonald's is genius when it comes to marketing. They are not called *Happy Meals* for nothing. Have you ever seen the commercials with their catchy little jingle at the end, "I'm Loving It"? They are programming your mind to anchor in positivity and love to their brand. This is what most successful marketing companies do. They want to stimulate the pleasure centers in your brain. Just like the beer commercials I explained earlier in this book.

As Jack was carrying his "Holy Grail" chipmunk around, he pushed on the top of the toy's head and out came the catchy little jingle, "I'm Loving It". "Pure genius", is what I remember thinking. After shaking my head in disbelief I then realized what was really going on in my son's mind.

As you can see in the diagram on the next page, Jack is getting programmed to believe that McDonald's is the place to go to feel good about eating. Whenever you build the synapse to have to eat a particular food to feel good it may lead to being an emotional eater, which is unhealthy. It can lead to having an addiction to food. Food is meant to nurture our bodies, not inhibit them. Would you fill up your car with fuel that made it spit and sputter down the road? I don't care how cheap the fuel was, you would not do it

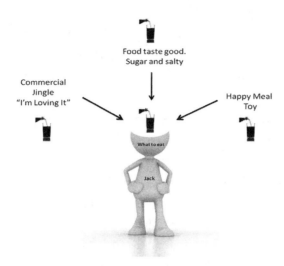

Food taste good.
Sugar and salty

Commercial
Jingle
"I'm Loving It"

Happy Meal
Toy

What to eat

Jack

because your family depends on your car. You paid a lot of money for your vehicle so you take care of it. You get the tires rotated, the oil changed and keep up the maintenance schedule so the car will last as long as it can.

Several years ago, the news did a story about a 91 year old woman who owned the same V8 Mercury Comet for the past 46 years. It had the original engine block with 562,000 + miles. She said that nothing was too good for her "chariot" and that she took care of this car like it was her own child. She religiously kept up on all the necessary mechanical service the car needed. She even went on to boast that she has gotten it up to 120 mph on several occasions. She's 91! Imagine if we all took as good care of our bodies as we do our vehicles.

I had a client we'll call Jane, who contemplated suicide on several occasions because her excess weight led to a severe case of depression. She confided to me that her whole life revolved around food. Her father was extremely overweight and they ate horribly all the time. Their meals consisted of processed food, fast food, snacks, pop and sweets. This was their way of life.

In the past Jane was an outstanding high school athlete excelling in softball, even making the varsity team as a freshman. However, there was one thing always hanging over her head and it was her weight. She would get comments from friends and family here and there about her weight and it would hurt. She wasn't getting bullied about it but she wasn't getting the dates and attention like other young ladies her age and it started to take a mental toll. Eventually, Jane's body began to fail and she started to experience chronic low back pain from being overweight. Her organs started to get stressed and her gallbladder had to be removed due to the years of abuse it sustained from an unhealthy lifestyle. Finally, she had a breakdown and her parents checked her into a mental health clinic which started her on smorgasbord of medications. Initially, she felt good after starting the medications, but as time went by, she found she was experiencing the same suicidal thoughts she had before and sometimes worse.

One of the medications prescribed was Ritalin (methylphenidate), an amphetamine-like prescription stimulant commonly used to treat Narcolepsy and Attention Deficit Hyperactivity Disorder (ADHD) in children and adults. Like many medications, Ritalin carries a laundry list of possible side effects. Occasionally, it is even possible to experience side effects that exhibit symptoms the drug is designed to treat.

Many think Ritalin is safe, or mild, because so many children use it. However, the government classifies the psychoactive drug with cocaine and morphine because it is *highly addictive*. *Drug Enforcement Agency classifies it as a Schedule II controlled Substance like cocaine.*

A review of 20-years of scientific literature on using stimulant medications, including Ritalin, to treat children with ADD and ADHD found a consensus: there is *no documented long-term benefit* (academic achievement or pro-social behavior) in using psychoactive drugs.[4]

This is what her mind looked like.

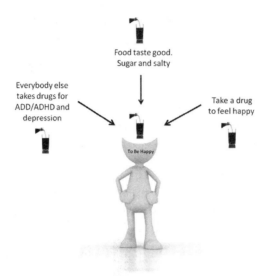

Since we live in an instant gratification society we want results now. Jane's doctors decided to treat the symptom rather than the underlying cause of why she was overweight and depressed to begin with, i.e. her family history of over eating and consuming junk food. They did not change anything in her environment except for adding drugs. Initially, the drugs made Jane feel great. Her parents were excited to see their little girl back, but little did they know it was building a belief system of, "When I am sad I need a drug."

After being on Ritalin and other anti-depressants for over a year, Jane started experiencing some of the side effects like severe depression and suicidal thoughts. They decided to wean her off of the drug. Unfortunately, she was already addicted to the Ritalin and this led to other addictions such as alcohol and drug abuse. In and out of mental institutions, Jane battled her weight and depression for several years. Finally, her father gave me a call to see if I could help.

I explained to him the environment she grew up in was one of the problems. As I shared with him the Universal Laws and how the mind works his eyes filled up with tears as he realized he was one of his daughter's problems and he never even knew it. I reassured him that many parents are doing the same destructive things without even realizing it, but it is never too late to change.

We laid out a plan not only for her but for him as well. After several months, they both have lost a combined weight of 100 pounds and are well on their journey to living a healthier more abundant life.

We can no longer turn a blind eye at the debacle that is happening with our youth. So many parents are turning to what is easy and convenient and they will drug their children for an instant result instead of looking at themselves and their child's environment. Again, I am not against medication. When used properly I think it is fantastic, but I am against the OVERMEDICATION that is happening in our society. We have no idea of what the long term damage will be from these medications. Most of them have not been adequately researched for long term side effects.

When you see teenagers contemplating suicide because of the mental baggage they carry from their past, it makes you realize how critical environment is when raising your own children. Remember, God had entrusted us with one of the most important responsibilities— being a successful parent. We must build positive belief systems which will enable our children to succeed in whatever they decide to do with their lives.

I am sure many of you have the feeling of guilt in one form or another. I know I did when my child mirrored my behavior. It is okay. It is not your fault unless you do not use and apply the tools you have been presented with in this book. The damage can be reversed. It just depends on how dark their cola is. The darker the cola, the longer it may take.

Just like you use affirmations to reprogram your mind, you also do the same with programming your child's mind.

Some of the affirmations I have my sons repeat are;

- I'm smart!
- I'm a hard worker!
- I'm a leader!
- Money comes easy to me!
- Whatever I put my mind to I can achieve!
- I'm a genius!
- I'm athletic!
- I have a patient mind!
- I have a big heart!
- I fall down seven, I get up eight!
- I'm beautiful inside and out!

Look at the diagram below to see the magic in this!

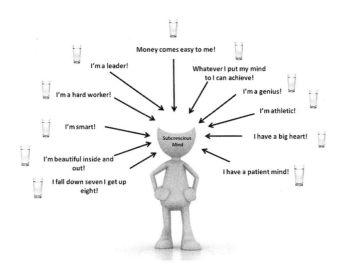

You can make up as many affirmations as you wish. Every day, as much as I can, I have my son say them out loud. I say one and he repeats it. Also, you just don't say them. You have to say them with high energy!

Anthony Robbins, a life coach and a man I admire, talks about getting into a state when you want to make an instant change in your mind. The state he describes is a *Gold Medal Winning Olympic* state. Think about this for a moment. To be the number one person in the world in a specific event is pretty special. Champions train their whole lives for one event and then they have to compete against others who have done the same. Whoever is on top of their game on that particular day is crowned the gold medalist and their names will be forever etched in the record books. Imagine what this must feel like. How proud and good they must feel. Sometimes they resonate these feelings so strongly that you and I, from half way across the world, will get goose bumps watching them on TV.

Did you hear what I just said about the goose bumps? How many times have you watched something on TV, YouTube, etc. and gotten the goose bumps or cried tears of joy? This is the state I need you in when you do these affirmations to not only for yourself but also with your children. *This* is resonation people! *This* is speaking God's language!

I'm not saying that I want you to start balling your eyes out in front of your children and grabbing them while you're sobbing and saying, "We have to do your affirmations!" That would surely freak them out. I want you to make it fun and exciting! When my sons do their affirmations I have them jump up and down and say it with excitement. They are anchoring in positive energy while they are instilling these new belief systems. You have to make sure these belief systems are surrounded by an impenetrable titanium wall. If you do not, the first time your child gets challenged the belief system may crumble.

Sometimes I will ask my children if they want to do their affirmations and one of them will stubbornly say, "No, I don't want to." Do not force them to do it. You must use power, not force. I usually say, "Okay, but I'm going to do them." Then I start doing them and usually they join in, but even if they do not say them, they are still hearing me do it, which pumps the clear water into their mind.

The best part of this exercise is you are actually pouring water into your own limiting cola belief system while you build their minds. You are hitting two birds with one stone.

I remember hanging out with my kids on a fall afternoon and Jack, my oldest, was tearing up the place having a great time when he tripped over a pillow and fell face first into the ground. He immediately got up and said, "I fall down seven, I get up eight." Thank goodness I wasn't on film because I was over in the corner fist pumping like I'd just scored the game winning touchdown in the Super Bowl because I knew the affirmation had taken root into his mind.

Life is easy in the beginning because all you have to deal with is the child's immediate environment like monitoring what they watch on TV, monitoring what you say and how you act during situations and monitoring the babysitter. In my situation, I was fortunate enough to have my parents close by to babysit.... but remember who programmed you. You need to also get them on board with this program. If everybody in the child's environment is programming their mind with positive mind food then your child will have a nice tall clear glass of pure abundant belief systems to take them farther then we could have ever achieved in every aspect of their life.

Life is good until they enter daycare or start school. Then it is a constant battle of the "cola/water" wars. When your child goes to school eight hours out of the day they are bombarded with the negative belief system of other kids, teachers, parents etc. When they come home you must in essence deprogram them with the use of affirmations.

Some people will read this and say, "This is a little excessive, don't you think?"

Let me tell you a story. When I was in college I knew an older woman who was an elementary school gym teacher. She was about four or five years from retirement. Every time I spoke with this woman she had nothing but horrible things to say about her job. She used to always vent about how bad her students were and how horrible it was to put up with them every day.

I used to try to get her to see the positives of the situation, but she wouldn't have any of it. I remember saying to her, "Hey, the school year is almost done and you will get a new batch of kids next year."

Her reply was, "Those kindergarteners coming up are just as rotten as this group of kids."

As I recall, gym time should be a fun time, especially at the elementary level. It should be a time where kids anchor in the belief system of "Exercise is fun and is a great way to burn some excess energy". Do you think the 100's of children she sees every year are getting good clear water into their belief systems or two liters of cola every day!

How many children's minds does she contaminate each day? Making matters worse, I'm sure that the parents are not aware of what is happening at school. Even if they are, do they have the tools to deprogram the filth that is attacking their children's minds on a daily basis?

I know many teachers, who are very passionate about the kids they interact with. They nurture the kids and have nothing but great things to say about their jobs and how much they love what they do. I am sure this type of thinking makes up 95% of the profession, but what about the other 5%?

These negative situations happen every day across our planet. It is like a horrible cancer that is metastasizing within our youth, our future! It is time to draw a line in the sand and do what is right—not what we have been programmed to do. It is time for a change!

Many people who start this new journey of "awareness" of one's thoughts and actions will sometimes feel a sense of guilt because of the affect their behavior and the negative environment [which they did not monitor] has had on their children just like the father of my client who was overweight. Remember, guilt is the worst of all the negative emotions and it must be squashed immediately. Many times parents will voice their guilt to me especially when they have teenage children. I simply explain that

No matter where you are in life right now, no matter who you are, no matter how old you are, it is never too late to be who you are meant to be.
—Unknown

Just start the process of pouring the new pure belief systems into your teenager's minds. It may be difficult at first and uncomfortable to them but you must start somewhere. It may just take a little longer for them to solidify a new belief into their mind, just like you and me who have gallons of cola in our minds. Let them read this book and learn from it also. It is never too late to start this journey. You can start having a positive impact immediately on your children's mind.

CALL TO ACTION EXERCISE
1. Start the process of doing affirmations with your children on a daily basis. Make it fun and exciting for them. This process

is a marathon, not a sprint. Consistency is needed here until it becomes habitual.

2. The age of your child will determine how dark their cola is. If you have a teenager, do not allow them to sink into old limiting behaviors and attitudes. If they say something negative, correct it with a positive affirmation. Keep them resonating high at all costs. Patience is important in these situations. Do not expect them to buy into this new journey immediately. Let time run its course and they will start to see the value of resonating high in their lives. You must first lead by example!

3. If you are starting to feel guilty about the way you have been raising your kids, STOP! Start the process of forgiving yourself by using the Forgiveness Letter you learned about in previous chapters. Do not allow yourself to feel guilty. Research has been done testing the sweat of different people experiencing a variety of positive and negative emotions. When they tested the sweat of people experiencing a negative emotion it was very acidic. Guilt is one of the most acidic of all the emotions. The sweat of people experiencing positive emotions was alkaline. Scientists have discovered that the bodily fluids of healthy people are alkaline (high pH) whereas the body fluids of sick people are acidic (low pH). Making sure your body has a balanced pH is a major step towards well-being and greater health. Our bodies must maintain a slightly alkaline pH to be optimal. How many times have you been upset and gotten an upset stomach? When you are acidic it puts unnecessary stress on your organs, systems and cells. Why do you think you get sick when you are stressed? Stress taxes the immune system and makes your body more vulnerable to illness. Have you ever heard of someone having a heart attack when they are

stressed? Your body is like an electrical outlet. When you have too many appliances plugged into one outlet, what happens? It can overload the circuit and blow a fuse. This is what happens when you overload your body with trauma, toxins and negative thoughts. To live a healthy optimal life you must unplug some of those unnecessary hindrances. Resonating high allows you to remove some of those plugs. If you don't resonate high your body will malfunction and your very life may be at stake!

Chapter Seven

CRAB MENTALITY

Your career and life will change for the better when you learn to surround yourself with positive people and keep the negative ones away.
—Unknown

According to the website wisegeek.com, "The term *crab mentality* is used to describe a kind of selfish, short-sighted thinking which runs along the lines of, "If I can't have it, neither can you." This term is widely used among Filipinos, who use it specifically to refer to people who pull other people down, denigrating them rather than letting them get ahead or pursue their dreams. As a general rule, the accusation of having a crab mentality is a poor reflection on someone's personality.

This concept references an interesting phenomenon which occurs in buckets of crabs. If one crab attempts to escape from a bucket of live crabs, the other crabs will pull it back down rather than allow it to get free. Sometimes, the crabs seem almost malicious, waiting until the fleeing crab has almost escaped before yanking it back into the pot. All of the crabs are undoubtedly aware of the fact that their fate is probably not going to be very pleasurable, so people are led to wonder why they pull each other back into the bucket, instead of congratulating the clever escape artist."[5]

How many times have we woken up, looked at ourselves in the mirror and said to our beautiful reflection, "This is the day I am going to change! I'm starting over today! Today is the beginning of my new life!"

We take this new found confidence and go meet the world head on like everybody else, but today we are going to do it differently because we have a new purpose, goal, or vision. As the hours go by you feel as if you have a new lease on life. With your head held up high you start to walk around with a chip on your shoulder. Throughout the day "crabs", I mean people start to notice there is something different about you and come to investigate the "new you". You allow them in on your goals and dreams and instead of joy and encouragement, you hear negativity. Every negative comment feels like stomach punch from a heavyweight boxer, sucking the air out of you. At the end of the day you feel as if you went 15 rounds with Mike Tyson.

Why does this happen? It is Crab Mentality. Remember, people's egos are so comfortable with their own environment that they do not welcome change. When you or somebody else decides to disrupt the herd mentality, you are immediately seen as a threat and must be brought back to what is considered "normal". Again, let's look at the diagram on the next page.

Do some of these comments ring a bell? I know they do in my life. This is why it is so important to constantly surround yourself with people who are going to further you and not beat you down.

I always love hearing stories of people who have thought outside the box. This is where the human spirit is at its best and where you feel the most alive. So many of us want to do it but we fear the unknown

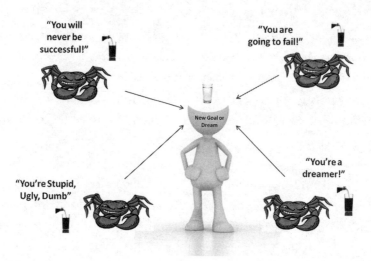

consequences of what other people will say. Below is a personal story and lesson learned from thinking outside my own box.

Each day is a gift and you never know how you can make a difference to someone you have wronged.

One day, when I was in 7th grade, we were playing softball in gym class. Like many students in school you have your athletes and your nonathletic kids. This particular game was evenly matched and the score was very close. It was the bottom of the last inning and all we had to do was get one more out and we would win. However, the bases were loaded so any mistake we made would guarantee them a win. I was the pitcher and when I delivered the softball the batter hit a slow ground ball that trickled to our second baseman. Anybody with the athletic capabilities of a sloth could have easily fielded the ground ball and made the last out. Our second baseman, however, wasn't blessed with athletic ability and he missed it, two runs scored off the error, thus ending the game and we lost.

In the heat of the moment I yelled at him in anger, "How could you miss such an easy ball? Stay away from me Jason (not his real name) if you know what is good for you because I'm going to kill you."

Since he was now easy prey for the blame, other kids followed my bad example and started to harp on him too. I walked off the field still steaming from the loss.

Little did I know, Jason had a meltdown and ran home from school after gym. Several hours later I was called to the principal's office and there was Jason's mother sobbing. The principal sat me down along with others who engaged in similar threats and told us Jason was contemplating suicide because of what happened in gym class earlier in the day. He was literally scared to come back to school because he feared the repercussions he might suffer at the hands of me and my fellow classmates. He thought his life was going to be over so he might as well help it along. I was floored. It was only a softball game and it was already a distant memory in my own mind, but not in Jason's.

What I didn't know was Jason had a real tough life and his father was no longer in the picture. The principal pulled me aside and said, "Garrett, *bad stuff* has happened to him in the past and he doesn't need or want you to know what the bad stuff is. You are a leader and kids look up to you. Give this kid a break and help him out."

I reassured his mother that nothing would happen to Jason and I would have his back. From then on I watched Jason's back without him even knowing it. When other kids would start bullying him in their own little way I would take them aside and have some words with them. After a few of my "interventions" they left him alone.

Several years passed and I became a big time football player in my school. My stardom grew even more when I signed with WMU my senior year. My life was rolling but I never forgot what happened in 7th grade. I would see Jason walking through the halls and I would always say hello if our paths crossed but something still bothered me inside when I saw him. He always looked like a broken dog when our paths would cross. He looked as if he was still carrying around the bricks of humiliation.

Then it hit me. I apologized to his mother but I never officially apologized to him personally. My ego immediately reared up and said, "You are a big time football player. You don't need to apologize for your mistake. You are a warrior and what you said was in the heat of battle. You were right in criticizing him. It is survival of the fittest, Garrett!"

I put my ego in timeout and walked up to him and pulled him aside. He looked as if a brisk wind would blow him over. He was looking down and I said, "Hey man, I know you probably don't' remember this but in 7th grade I got on you about a softball game we lost. I never apologized for my actions toward you and I just wanted to say how sorry I am for taking it out on you. It wasn't your fault. Will you accept my apology?"

He looked up from the ground and with tears in his eyes said, "Yes, I forgive you and thank you. This really was big of you to do."

Boy, did I feel like a donkeys butt for not apologizing earlier. I never knew what happened to Jason after we graduated, but I know our paths crossed for me to learn a valuable lesson on life, which is each day is a gift from God! Don't forget to say "I'm sorry" to the people you've wronged" An apology goes a long way.

Whenever you dare to be great you will always have the crabs who are trying to bring you down. When I told some of my friends about what had happened years earlier with Jason they just laughed and said, "Who cares what he feels like. You're better than him. He's a geek." I could have taken the easy way out and not apologized to this kid but I would still be carrying the guilt (worst of the negative emotions) around in the back of my mind, limiting me in unforeseen ways. This is why you must always do what is right rather than just what everybody else around you is doing.

Thank God I had a great support group on my journey when I made the decision to be a Division I football player. This is what my mind consisted of when I was trying to achieve my goal of earning a Division I scholarship.

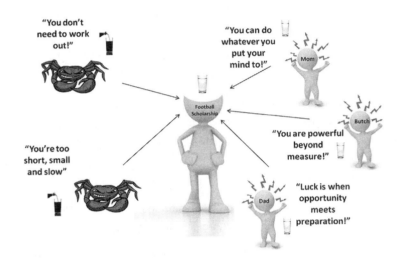

As you can see my mind was bombarded with positive and negative thoughts from all sides. If you want to make a change on your life it is very important to eliminate as many crabs from your environment as possible. When you have a positive environment, along with ammunition from your own affirmations, anything is possible. We can attract whatever we desire most and enrich our lives full of the abundance of God.

This is why it is so important to keep up with your children's affirmations. As they grow older they spend more and more time away from you and can easily get cola poured into their mind. You must protect as much of their environment as possible. You must monitor their usage on the internet, TV, friends and video games. I remember growing up with *Nintendo* games like *Super Mario Brothers* and *Contra*.

Have you see what is available today? It is amazing how far video games have come in 20 years.

One day my cousin brought his Play Station 3 over and I was playing one of his *First-Person Shooter* (FPS) games. This is a video game genre that centers on gun and projectile weapon-based combat through first-person perspective, i.e., the player experiences the action through the eyes of the character. I am very competitive. Like many of you I want to win. This is why video games are very addictive to me. I do not want to put down the controller until I have conquered the game. If I am not careful I'll find myself playing for several hours straight trying to beat the game. On one particular day after 20 minutes into the game, I felt like my heart was beating through my chest and my breathing was fast and erratic. When I finally beat the game, the character that I was playing saved all his men but was mortally wounded. [Remember, you are playing through the eyes of the character.] What I was seeing was my men, whom I'd just saved, coming up to me screaming with a look of desperation, "Hang in there! You're going to make it! Don't quit! We need a medic!"

While they were screaming words of encouragement there was powerful instrumental music playing in the background. When I say powerful, I mean the kind of instrumental music you heard at the end of *Braveheart* when William Wallace was being executed or at the end of *Gladiator* when Maximus was dying. The music literally gives you chills throughout your entire body and sometimes will even bring a tear to your eye. As the music was playing, my character's eyes started to blink and everything was starting to get blurry on the TV screen. The last thing before the entire screen went black was the final words of one of my men sadly saying, "He's dead."

As the game ended and the credits rolled, I noticed I was sweating and my eyes were filled with tears. It was as if the game I was playing was actually real. My mind could not tell the difference.

I put down the controller and thought to myself, "Holy cow, how many kids are playing these types of games and the parents don't even realize it?"

These games are rated, *M for Mature* for a reason. They are very violent and depict the horrors of war and in some cases how horrible the human race can be. These games have no place in a developing child's mind. I know of a young child whose parents are going through a rough time. In many of these tough situations the parents become selfish and will forget the needs of their children. In this particular case it was easier to put their son in front of a video game to keep him busy instead of finding more constructive things for him to do. He ran up to me one day and was very happy. He proudly explained to me that his parents just got him the best gift in the world—a very popular video game similar to the one I just described in the previous paragraphs depicting the horrors of war. It was called *Modern Warfare 3*, rated M for Mature. HE WAS FIVE!

I cringe every time I hear of a parent getting their young child these games because they are too busy to parent or they are not aware of the content of the games. Either way, in my opinion, this is bad parenting.

We must constantly be aware of what is continuingly filling our children's minds. Again, I am not trying to be a poster boy for the "Anti Gaming" movement. I enjoy playing video games, but if not monitored appropriately, these violent games can be just as dangerous as the over consumption of drugs and alcohol.

CALL TO ACTION EXERCISE

1. If you want to shorten the time it takes for manifestation to occur then you must limit all of the crabs in your environment. If they bring you down and do not support your new journey then you have two choices, either drop them or decide not to

share your new goals and dreams with them. If they are limiting your children in anyway then the answer is obvious, they must go. You must surround yourself with high resonating people who will be with you and your children on this new path. The hardest part of limiting the crabs from your environment is if they are close family members like your mother or father. If this is the case then get them this book so they will have a clear picture of where you are coming from. If they still choose not to change because of ego, then you must limit them as much as possible in your new clear environment. I'm not saying to disown your parents, but you must monitor the situation closely, especially if children are involved. There are always special occasions and holidays throughout the year you must attend with family members. This is fine as long as you go into the situation with your eyes open and control it. You control it by preparing your mind with affirmations. You can use affirmations such as:

"I'm so happy and grateful now that I have a meaningful and passionate relationship with my family."

"I'm so happy and grateful now that I look at the positive in every situation."

This allows you to associate positivity with your family. Remember, your consistent thoughts are what you attract and if you associate negativity with your family then you will bring out the worst in them. Positive affirmations allow you to anchor in high resonation with your family and this will bring out the best in them. Even if it doesn't bring out the best in them the affirmations will bulletproof your mind so you don't fall into the old behaviors and attitudes that are far less than what you and your children deserve. Either way you win.

2. Whenever you dare to be great, you will feel resistance from your environment. Many times in my practice my patients have been my greatest teachers about life. One particular patient sticks out in my mind about persistence. This gentleman is in his 50's and his body is chiseled like a Greek statue. This summer he plans on riding his road bike down the west coast just for fun. Over the past year he has been training for this adventure. When Mike comes in we usually chat about life and events that have happened in our past, which have shaped us into who we are now. One day during his Chiropractic adjustment he shared with me a great story on life. The conversation went as followed: "Yesterday, I commuted to work, rode with the evening biking group and then commuted home (just shy of 50 miles). During all the rides, I just felt slow on the bike, yet I know that I was putting a lot of energy into the ride. Even though I was riding hard and sweating with an elevated heart rate, I just could not get my speed up. So, I just geared down and spun. It was one heck of a cardio workout. Finally, being a Scientist, about 10 miles from home I asked, "What is different today?" I got off my bike and looked it over. Well unbeknownst to me, the rear brake was rubbing on my back tire just enough to provide resistance. When I released the brake, got back on the bike, it was wonderful…energy and effort translated to speed and the remainder of the ride was beautiful."

So, what is the life lesson here…

"Where else in my life am I riding with my brakes on?"

"Where else am I holding back and what is holding me back?"

"Where else is there resistance in my life that I can release?"

"What stuff am I holding on to that is taking way too much energy to carry forward?"

I know that at the end of the day, it is my responsibility to ask the questions and figure it out. As Mr. Carnegie reminded us, decide just how much anxiety a thing is worth and refuse to give it more and then, let it go!

Thanks Mike and keep enjoying the ride of life!

Chapter Eight

GOALS

*"Obstacles are what you see when
you lose sight of your goal"*
— **Nadiatul**

Since I live in the Midwest, would it make sense for me to plant grapefruit or orange trees in my backyard? No, of course not. I think we will all agree they would probably do much better in a warmer climate. If you want to have a successful business selling ice cream, would you have better luck selling it in Antarctica or in Miami Beach, Florida? The answer is obvious. My point is you must first make your goals realistic.

Don't get me wrong, I want you to shoot for the stars! I once read that it is better to throw a rock at the moon and hit an eagle than to throw a rock at an eagle and hit the ground. By all means reach for the stars but if you are 85 years old I do not think it is the appropriate time for you to try to play in the NFL. We may laugh at this but this is how many people approach their goals. They set impossible goals for themselves and when they don't achieve them in a timely manner, they get discouraged and pour more cola into their already established belief of "low self- esteem". This leads to anxiety and depression (a negative resonation). The best way to achieve goals is to make them realistic and achievable in the beginning. Then, as your confidence grows you can set more ambitious goals.

There are some people out there who seem to be able to achieve their objective no matter what it is. I think this is great. Unfortunately this is also rare. Most people will start working toward a goal and after encountering a few obstacles give up, make excuses or blame others for their failures. They unconsciously end up passing limiting beliefs on to their children by telegraphing the belief that, "If it's hard then I will just quit or just blame everybody else when things don't turn out the way I wanted." Don't forget…. whenever you feel as though you need to point your finger at somebody or something else as the reason you did not succeed, you need to remember there are three fingers pointing back at you.

In the beginning, when setting up realistic goals, you must first crawl before you can walk. For example, if you've been leading a sedentary life and decide you want to lose 35 pounds and be in great physical condition, don't make the unrealistic goal of working out twice a day, seven days a week for the next year. You will probably fail, thus pouring more cola in your mind. Instead, make it a goal to work out once per day three times a week for three months. If you stay consistent and meet your goal you can increase the workouts to four or five days a week. After you come up with a realistic goal, you'll need to decide if this goal is what you really want to accomplish. Do you have the desire? If you do not, choose another goal. There will be challenges along the way and if you do not have the desire to accomplish the goal then you will quit. This will pour more cola into your "low self- esteem" limiting belief.

I know this has happened repeatedly in my own life. I have always wanted to compete in a full *Ironman*. A full Ironman consists of a 2.4 mile swim, 112 mile bike ride, topped off with a beautiful 26.2 mile run. I have run several half Ironman's, but always wanted to do the full. Notice how I said, "wanted". If I would have said, "desired," then I probably wouldn't be typing this story right now because I would have already accomplished the goal of finishing a full Ironman.

To finish a full Ironman it takes 100% commitment. You have to train for hours throughout the day and balance your time between workouts, job, family, friends, etc. There have been several occasions when I have signed up (over $600 non-refundable entry fee for each race) and after several weeks come to the conclusion in my mind that I don't have the time right now and then I make the decision to not do it. I feel relieved when I finally make this decision, because it frees up my time, but I have to be careful with how my mind reacts to quitting because I have the belief that quitters do not make it in this world. If I am not careful I may pour more cola into my mind fueling a negative belief system that I am a quitter and this in turn will limit me in some area of my life.

Like most things in life, the best way to avoid a negative situation is to prevent it from happening. Unfortunately, most of us have to wait to have a "heart attack" before we change our lifestyle patterns to prevent the heart attack from happening. This is why I am warning you about the difference between wanting and desiring a specific goal. If you don't have the desire to do whatever is necessary to accomplish the goal then don't even put it in your mind. In my situation I had to analyze and explain to myself that my children and wife are more important right now and I should be spending more time with them and not going off on some heat of the moment escapade to further the ego within myself.

Once you have figured out if you have the desire to achieve your goal(s) you must get it down on paper and assign a timeline for each goal. Let me stop right there and clear something up. Many people ask will ask what the difference is between a goal and belief.

Merriam-Webster Online Dictionary defines a belief as:

1. a state or habit of mind in which trust or confidence is placed in some person or thing.
2. something believed; *especially* : a tenet or body of tenets held by a group.
3. conviction of the truth of some statement or the reality of some being or phenomenon especially when based on examination of evidence.[1]

Merriam-Webster Online Dictionary defines a goal to be,

1: The end toward which effort is directed.[6]

I want to lose 35 pounds is a goal. I'm so happy and grateful now that I am the healthiest I have ever been is a belief. You must have both in order for you to maximize your effort and achieve your goal. Anybody can lose 35 pounds quickly. Cut off your leg and you will surpass the goal of losing 35 pounds. Obviously, this is not the healthy way to do it. This is why you must combine your goal with the belief that it has already happened. When you combine a belief along with a goal this makes you a powerful magnet to attract what you want most in your life and keep you on the road to consistently taking actions towards your desired outcome.

Here are some examples of beliefs and goals that go together.

Belief: I'm so happy and grateful now that money comes to me in increased quantities from multiple sources on a continued basis.

Goals: I'm so happy and grateful now that I net $8,000/month or more. I'm so happy and grateful now that I am saving $10,000/ year or more for retirement. I'm so happy and grateful now that I am investing in one real estate property/year or more to get rental income, etc.

Belief: I'm so happy and grateful now that I am living life to the fullest.

Goals: I'm so happy and grateful now that my wife and I visited Mexico and explored the Mayan ruins. I'm so happy and grateful now that I have climbed the Grand Tetons in Wyoming. I'm so happy and grateful now that I have been skydiving, etc.

Belief: I'm so happy and grateful now that I am the best athlete I can be.

Goals: I'm so happy and grateful now that I made All State in Soccer. I'm so happy and grateful now that I can run the 40 yard dash in 4.68 sec. I'm so happy and grateful now that I have earned a full Division I scholarship in football/volleyball/basketball/hockey. I'm so happy and grateful now that I weigh 195 pounds, etc.

You must first establish the belief in yourself before you set out to accomplish your goals. Affirmations, along with a few other techniques I will share with you in a minute, allow you to trick your mind into thinking the outcome, which you are trying to attract, has already happened. In essence, you must fake it before you make it. This makes you a magnet for what you desire most. This allows the time it takes to accomplish your goal (Universal Law of Gender) to be shorter. Affirmations are the *Miracle Grow* to your *seeds* allowing them to grow faster and larger than if you didn't use fertilizer.

Since we all live in an instant gratification society and we want everything *now*, it is nice to have some extra fertilizer for the mind to help shorten the time it takes to accomplish our goals. Using affirmations along other goal achieving techniques accomplishes this. Along with using affirmations you can also utilize visualization, vision boards and goal cards.

Remember reading in previous chapters about how you must keep yourself at a high positive resonation to attract the things you desire most? Visualization is a great tool to accomplish this. Like many great athletes I used the power of visualization all the time. Let me prove to you how powerful visualization is and how you can "trick" your mind into thinking what you are visualizing is real.

Imagine yourself sitting in your living room on a hot and humid summer day. You are sweating profusely and your mouth is parched from the dehydration that has set in from the heat. You decide you need something to quench your thirst. You get up and walk into your kitchen and open the door to your fridge. All you see sitting on the top shelf is a bowl filled with huge yellow fresh lemons. Reach in and pick up a lemon. As you run your fingertips over the smooth surface you notice the waxy yellow texture. Squeeze the lemon slightly and feel the presence of fresh juice inside. Grab a sharp knife and cut the lemon in two halves. As you cut notice how your nose picks up its powerful ripe citrus fragrance. Pick up one of the halves and feel the cool juice running down your hand. Now bring the lemon up to your mouth, open wide, and take a huge bite into that juicy lemon. Really sink your teeth into it. Now suck the lemon and taste the poignant sour flavor of the lemon as the pulp hits your tongue and explodes throughout your entire mouth. Notice how your eyes squint as you bite into it and you make that universal sour face.

Did you experience a physiological response from what you just read? Did your mouth start to salivate? Did your eyes squint and make the sour face? Most people who read this will have some sort of physical reaction to it. What happened? Obviously, the lemons are not real because you imagined them but your mind could not tell the difference. This is how visualization works. You trick your mind into thinking that what you want to accomplish has already happened thus allowing you to be a magnet for what you want to attract.

In the 1930's, Judd Blaslotto, Ph.D at the University of Chicago did a study splitting people into three groups and testing each group to see how many free throws they could make. After this, he had the first group practice free throws every day for an hour. The second group just visualized themselves making free throws. The third group did nothing. After 30 days, he tested them again. The first group improved by 24%. The second group improved by 23% without even touching a basketball. The third group did not improve, which was expected. Imagine if there was a fourth group combining practice and visualization. I'm sure the improvement would have been even higher.

You can utilize visualization with every goal you want to achieve. Have fun with it and enjoy the feelings it will produce. I was working with a client, who like many people, would try to lose weight only to come up short and then gain it all back again. She had heard that I might be able to help her lose those unwanted 45 pounds. She explained to me that in the past she would start her weight loss journey with determination and after several months she would lose 20-30 pounds and feel great. For some reason after she would reach this milestone of losing more than half of her goal weight she would fall back into the old limiting behavior and attitudes of over eating and skipping workouts. She always ended up gaining all of her weight back, if not more, and this would lead to depression.

I explained to her that she was doing everything right in the beginning, but she was coming up short because she never really imagined what she would feel like at her goal weight. After a moment of thought, she started to tear up and confessed she was afraid to allow herself to imagine what it would feel like because of the possibility of letting not only herself down but her husband also. I explained to her that in fact, the total opposite would occur. This revelation allowed her to get over the hump and stay motivated during the challenging times. She just needed to start, along with her daily workout schedule and eating right, to also utilize the most important tool she had, which was her mind. I told her to close her eyes and visualize herself at her goal weight and let her thoughts drift to how sexy and alive she would feel looking at herself in the mirror. I told her to then glance over her shoulder and notice that her husband would not be able to take his eyes off of the new her. "Can you feel the desire in his eyes for you?" is what I asked her.

She said, "Yes, and I have chills all over my body."

I explained to her that this was the resonation she must be in as much as possible throughout the day. Whenever she was thinking of cheating on her diet or skipping a workout she must go through this fantasy in her mind. I told her to take the fantasy as far as she wanted, but she had to make sure she took the action steps each day of eating right and exercising to allow this fantasy to come true.

Several months later she was down below her goal weight and happy as ever. Not only is she feeling fantastic, but her husband and daughter jumped on the bandwagon and they are almost down to their goal weight. This is what God wants! He not only wants you to achieve your goals and dreams but to inspire others to do the same. This is serving humanity and paying it forward.

When you visualize and actually give yourself the chills then you know you are resonating with God and are on your way to attract whatever outcome you desire. Visualization is especially helpful when you are having a bad day and don't feel like working towards your goals. You can instantly snap yourself out of the negative resonation with five minutes of visualization, just like my client did with her weight loss.

When I visualize I listen to certain types of music, which inspire me. I visualize when I work out, on my way to work, and especially before I go to bed. I have read that the last thing you think about before you fall asleep is what your mind plays over and over again while you sleep. What a great opportunity to make sure you think of something positive so you can dump good clear water into your mind thousands of times throughout your night of slumber. Using the power of visualization allows you to have something at the end of the tunnel to constantly look forward to and keep you focused on taking the necessary action steps each day towards your goal.

Let me make a very important point here, a thought without action is a wish. You must take action, no matter how small, everyday towards your desired outcome. If you are visualizing each day and not working towards your goal you are simply day dreaming. You must take action. You have to earn what you are trying to achieve.

Another tool you can utilize is a *vision board*. A vision board is where you put everything you want to accomplish. Hang it up where you will see it the most throughout the day. You can put it anywhere. I have had people put it on dashboards, bathroom mirrors, in their office etc. You can have pictures of your dream house, the car you desire, where you want to travel, money, your dream body with a picture of your face on it, etc. John Aassaraf, a famous spiritual entrepreneur, utilized vision boards during his climb to ultra-success. He shares the story of making a vision board, years before his success, which he hung in his office and he would consciously and subconsciously look at throughout the day. Four years passed and he was in the process of moving into his new dream house. While he was unpacking, one of his children was sitting on a box and asked his father what was inside the box. He walked over, opened it and explained to him that this was some of his old office stuff from years ago. He pulled out his old vision board and then realized the very house he just bought was on the vision board he made four years ago.

The last tool I utilize is called a *goal card*. There are some rules when using this card. You need to be specific on the goals you desire and you must write them in a way that makes your mind think you have already achieved them. Such as:

- I'm so happy and grateful now that I am having a meaningful and passionate relationship with my wife and kids.
- I'm so happy and grateful now that I am a multimillionaire.
- I'm so happy and grateful now that I am netting $50,000/ month or more from my rentals.
- I'm so happy and grateful now that I weigh 195 pounds.
- I'm so happy and grateful now that my book is serving 1,000,000 people or more.
- I'm so happy and grateful now that I am having a meaningful and passionate relationship with God.

When analyzing these goals, you will notice they all are written in the present, as if they have already been met. You will also notice how some of them have the potential for more growth. There have been so many times in my life where I have limited myself. It wasn't until recently that I analyzed myself and realized it was the way I did my affirmations and how I would write my goals out.

For example I used to write my goals and say my affirmations like this:

- Goals for 5 years
- To be millionaire
- To be a successful entrepreneur
- To be a Happy Person
- To be a great father/husband
- To be 195 lbs

As you can see my goals were not very specific and they had no time constraints on them. They were all written out in the future tense "To be". When goals are written out this way it doesn't allow your mind to have a call to action. It essence, the mind is lazy because it can always put off achieving the goal until tomorrow. This is why you must write them out as if you already achieved the goal. This lights a fire in your mind to get to work.

When ancient Greek armies invaded foreign lands from the sea they often gave the order to "burn the boats" after their forces were ashore. This let the conquering army know there was no retreat. Their choice was to either win or die. When you write your goals out as if they've already happened, you are in essence burning the boats. This tells your mind you mean business; so let's get to work and start conquering the goals you set out to accomplish.

You never want to limit yourself. Why have a goal with set limits when you could possibly achieve more. You always want to leave room for more growth to happen. This is why competing with yourself is so much more important than competition with other people. When you compete against other people you actually can limit yourself. Just like the quote I used before, "It is better to throw a rock at the moon and hit an eagle then to throw a rock at an eagle and hit the ground." You may perceive the person you are competing against is the moon, but in all actuality they are the eagle. Never limit yourself. I have a quote written above my door that I read every time I leave my house which reads, "To Be The Best." It means to be my best in every aspect of my life. I strive every day to live each day like it's my last. I never know when I'm going to get called up to the "big leagues" and depart from this wonderful journey we call life. I want to make sure I leave my concrete foundation for my children to build the skyscraper of their dreams.

Once you have finished writing all of your goals on the card you need to carry it on your person at all times. You can choose to carry it in your pocket, bra, hat, wherever you are able to feel it on your person. I carry mine in my front right pocket. At night, you can even put it under your pillow or keep it in your pocket if you have one. I have read you are consciously aware of only 5% your environment. This means you are not consciously aware of 95% of your environment. What soaks up the 95%? Your subconscious mind does. So, with every movement you make or when your hand brushes up against your goal card throughout the day you are dumping good clear water into your mind. The diagram below shows the magic in what happens to your mind.

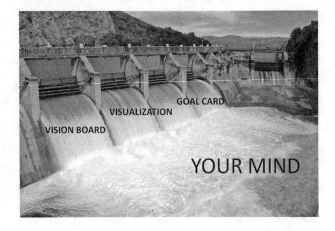

You are not pouring glasses of water into your mind anymore when you utilize the vision board, visualization and goal card. You are creating a constant waterfall! By using these techniques you are literally drowning your mind with pure positive resonation 24 hours/day, seven days/week. This makes you a powerful magnet to attract all the desires you ever imagined and in the least amount of time as possible.

You can even utilize the vision board, visualization and goal card with your children. For example, my son Jack, who is four years old, came to me one morning holding a piece of paper with advertisements for "Thomas & Friends" toys on it. He says, "Dada, I want you to get this for me."

I was excited because this was a perfect opportunity for me to start explaining the vision board to him and how he can earn the toy for himself. I went down on one knee and asked him, "Do you really desire this?"

He looked at me and with confusion and replied, "What is desire?"

I explained to him that desire means from the Father (God). When you desire something there are certain rules you must follow (Universal Laws) in order for you to manifest this toy. Of course, he had a look of confusion on his face [he's only four] but I always told myself I'd always tell my children the truth and not lie to them about anything. I want them to always have the belief system ingrained into their mind that their father tells the truth. I sat him down and said, "Jack, if you truly desire this toy then you must earn it. You won't have this toy tomorrow or even the next day, but in several weeks maybe. We are going to cut this picture out and start your first vision board. Every day if you do all the chores listed on the board you will get a star. If you earn 20 stars then when you wake up the next day this toy will be in the living room waiting for you."

His beautiful brown eyes lit up and got as big as saucers and he asked, "Will you get it for me, dada?"

"It may be me or mom, nana or papa but it all comes from God, hence the word desire, which means from the Father. If you do not accomplish all of your chores then you will not get a star. If you behave poorly, like not sharing with your brother, then you may get a star taken away."

He was fired up with excitement and anticipation for his reward. There were a few days where he didn't earn a star, but most of the time he did what he was supposed to and earned his star. Every night before bed, he placed a star on his vision board and he would count to see how many more he needed. As he would put the star on the board I would tell him to look at the picture and visualize with his mind that he was playing with the toy and how happy he felt while playing with it. He soaked it all in. He would look up and smile and say, "I love my toy."

Why did we do it before bed? So it would be the last thing on his mind and this thought would replay in his mind over and over again throughout his night's rest.

Here is my son Jack's first vision board.

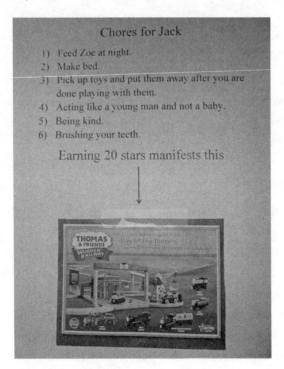

Chores for Jack

1) Feed Zoe at night.
2) Make bed.
3) Pick up toys and put them away after you are done playing with them.
4) Acting like a young man and not a baby.
5) Being kind.
6) Brushing your teeth.

Earning 20 stars manifests this

Many parents will ask, "Where do you draw the line with getting expensive extravagant toys for your kids?"

It is up to you as the parent. It is all relative. Donald Trump would probably get more expensive toys than I would but the lesson is universal. That is, when you work hard toward something, good things happen.

After he earned the 20th star on his board Jack stepped back and marveled at his accomplishment. You could see he was very proud of what he had done. He looked up at me and said, "Dad, that took a long time."

I kneeled down and said, "Jack, sometimes it takes a while for things to manifest but the longer and harder you work, the better it will feel when you've achieved your goal. Let's go to bed and tomorrow you will have your new toy."

I never saw him move so fast toward his sleeping bag (He was sleeping in our room on the floor at the time).

The next morning it was like Christmas for Jack. He woke up and when he came around the corner there was the toy he envisioned. It was a proud moment for me as a father knowing another solid belief system was instilled into his mind, which would carry him throughout his life.

Several weeks later Jack brought another picture of a toy he would like to earn which was more expensive and extravagant than the first. I did the same thing as before, which was cut out the picture and put it on his vision board and added more chores then the first. He also had to earn it over a longer period of time because this toy required 40 stars. He noticed he had to work harder than before and for a longer period of time and he looked up at me with those beautiful eyes and asked with confusion, "Why do I have more chores and why do I need more stars than before?"

I responded, "This toy is much bigger than your other one, isn't it?" He shook his head yes and agreed. "When you desire something greater, you have to earn it even more."

He let this comment process for a moment and then shook his head in agreement. For the next 40 days he worked toward his goal. When he put the final star on the board you could see the desire for his new extravagant toy in his eyes along with the anticipation of playing with it the very next morning. As soon as he awoke, he ran out to the living room to see the new toy which he had worked so hard to achieve. Waiting there for him was, however, a different toy. It was an extravagant toy but it was definitely a step down from what he worked so hard to achieve.

He started to cry. As a father, this hurt because I do not want to disappoint my child, especially when he worked so hard toward his goal. I knew, however, that this less than desirable outcome [from Jack's perspective] provided a huge life lesson for him as long as it was approached the right way.

I sat down next to him, gave him a hug and asked what was wrong (I wanted him to explain what he was feeling).

He looked up with tears in his eyes and said, "Dad, I did everything I was supposed to and I didn't get the toy I wanted."

I replied, "This is true, but you did receive a toy. Jack, sometimes you will go through life and you will work your heart and soul for something and sometimes you come up a little short and don't achieve your desired result. This is okay, but just like in this instance you'll still be rewarded for your hard work. When you work hard for something there will always be some sort of good that comes from it. There is no failure in life only lessons to be learned. You fall down seven…"

He responded, "I get up eight."

I hugged him and told him how proud I was of him and asked him if he wanted to work hard towards the toy he originally wanted and he put his hands on his hips and cocked his head to one side and said, "Of course Dad. I always get up eight."

CALL TO ACTION EXERCISE

1. Write out at least 10 goals you want to achieve in the next three years. Remember to start small and build upon the goals. Once you build the belief system of anything is possible then the sky is the limit for what you want to achieve. I have what is called the *Rule of 3*. It takes 0.3 seconds for a goal to enter your mind, 3 seconds to decide to achieve or not to achieve the goal, 3 minutes to write out an action plan to achieve the goal, 3 days to see if you need to reevaluate the goal, 3 weeks to reevaluate again. After 3 weeks you may already see some results toward your original goal—3 months to achieve small goals and 3 years to achieve large goals. You can change your goals at any time. If you find yourself not desiring something in a few months then change it. I adapt and change my goals all the time.

2. Start the process of utilizing the techniques I described in this chapter. Have fun with it. When you visualize, let the thoughts

come naturally to you. Do not feel anxiety or pressure when you visualize. Use this time to meditate on what you desire most.

3. Start introducing these concepts with your children. It is never too early to start vision boards, visualization and goal cards. The earlier the age the better.

Chapter Nine

PGD
(Post Goal Depression)

"As you reach your goals, set new ones. That is how you grow and become a more powerful person."
— **Les Brown**

As you are getting closer to achieving your goal(s), you must have an *Exit Action Plan* put into place following your accomplishment. If you don't have a plan put into place you may run the risk of going through what I call it *PGD* (Post Goal Depression).

You may be thinking to yourself, "How is this possible?"

Post goal depression has happened to me on several occasions and it wasn't until recently that I finally figured out what was going on. For over nine years, football wasn't just a game. It was my life. It was just as important to me as the blood running through my body. I lived and breathed it. I am not going to compare football to the horrors of war, because I won't dishonor my father and other veterans who have experienced war, but I feel football, along with other sports of that nature, is the closest thing you can get to war. The adrenalin

117

of playing in front of 85,000 people can be very addictive. Not only can the games be addictive but also the strong bonds created with teammates after going through workouts, practices, games, wins, losses, family deaths, injuries, etc. Camaraderie, similar to what's experienced in the military is created. When your football career is over and you find yourself out in the real world some athletes, [like me] go through a type of depression. I call it PGD (Post Goal Depression).

If you do not have an immediate Exit Action Plan put into place for when you achieve your goal or when you come up short you run the risk of this de-habilitating syndrome. Once you are experiencing PGD, you may find yourself falling into self-destructive behaviors (addictions) like binge drinking or other limiting behaviors to fill the void. This is what happened to me when my football career was over.

When I got the call from my agent that the Chicago Bears were going to cut me I felt as if I got hit in the gut. I felt that I'd let my family, fiancé and small hometown down. I had my bachelor's degree in criminal justice and already went through the police academy but my heart wasn't into being a police officer anymore. My life felt like it was going nowhere. I moved back home into my parents basement and took a low paying job installing manufactured homes. My original plan of making the NFL and my backup plan of becoming a police officer had fallen through. Two weeks prior to being cut, I was in Chicago living it up as a NFL athlete. Now, I was underneath a manufactured home digging in the dirt. After work I would come home to my parent's basement and go out and drown my sorrows in the bottle. I was depressed and I felt as though my life was falling apart. Two weeks after being cut I lost control of my truck [which I bought with my NFL bonus] and wrapped it around a tree.

Let's analyze what was going on in my mind at this time.

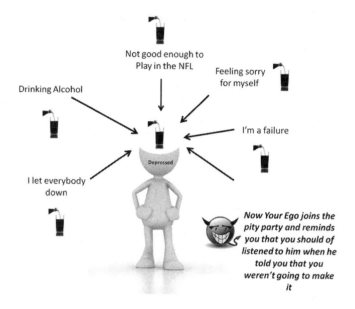

Every athlete loses sometime in their career, whether it is in a game or in life. These losses are critical to growth not only as an athlete but as a human being in order to keep striving to get better. There is many times when an undefeated team gets beaten by what is considered a "lower caliber" team. This is why I love sports. Any team always has a shot to win. Whoever shows up that day to play to win will have an opportunity to win. When an unbeaten team finally loses they have two ways to respond. One, make sure it never happens again and learn from the mistakes, allowing them to come back stronger from the experience, or two, they fall apart. I have experienced both situations in athletics and in life and I would rather be the person who rebounds and learns from the loss than the one who gives up. After I got cut from the Bears I chose door number two and fell apart. I was depressed, I totaled my truck, I was no longer an NFL athlete and if I wasn't careful I was on my way to becoming a "has been", which to me is somebody who always lives in the past and wants to relive the glory days. Every day you wake up can be a "glory day". You just have to decide to make it one.

Let's revisit the laws you have learned in this book and prove how your resonation is what you attract in your life. When you are constantly resonating negative feelings you will continue to attract more negativity. It wasn't enough that I got cut from the NFL and was working at a dead end job but then I started to drink to curb my low self-esteem. As we all know alcohol is a depressant, so it made me feel even more depressed. Since I was resonating low with the feelings of self-pity, sadness, embarrassment etc., I attracted more negativity and wrecked my truck. Let's look at the diagram on how this happened.

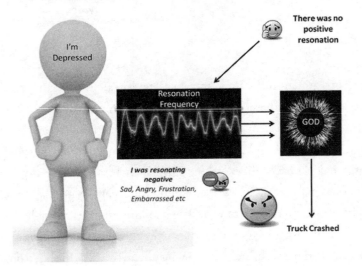

Many people will look at this graph and argue, "God is not going to give you something negative. This is the devil."

Remember, your own ego is the devil. God is the Universal Source and continues to give you what you think about most, positive or negative. How do I know this? Because He gave us the power of free will. It is not His fault when bad things happen in your life. Sometimes you must experience the bad to learn a lesson. The same lesson will appear over and over again until you learn from it. This is why you always have a choice in responding to what you perceive as a negative situation. If I had perceived that crashing my truck was a negative then my mind would have stayed in a low resonating field. If you stay negative you attract more negative. Instead, I perceived crashing my truck as a positive because it snapped me out of my vicious downward spiral. Once I realized how I was thinking and what I was doing to myself I started the process of crawling out my own hole of mediocrity by using the lessons taught throughout this book.

Have you ever had somebody confront you when you were wrong? Initially, what happens? You get defensive (ego/devil). If you are a rational person then you may analyze the situation and accept you were wrong and do whatever you need to do to right the situation by an apology or an act. If ego controls you then you won't admit you were wrong and continue to deny whatever you are trying to attract in your life (success, wealth, happiness, weight loss, love, passion, etc.).

PGD is another obstacle ego puts in front of you to hold you back from growing even more than you already did. My ego showed up again as I experienced PGD when I finished my first Marathon and Half Ironman. My PGD wasn't as severe as when football was over, but I still experienced a "what do I do now" feeling. This can all be prevented by having an *Exit Action Plan* put into place for after you achieve your goal.

The Exit Action Plan can be a type of maintenance schedule for the goal you just achieved or it can consist of building onto what you've already accomplished. A maintenance schedule is valuable for when your goal was to lose an "X" amount of weight. Once accomplished, your Exit Action Plan would consist of proper diet and exercise to maintain your current weight. If your goal was to make "X" amount of dollars then your Exit Action Plan could be to have another goal larger than the one you just accomplished. As long as you have several exit strategies put into place you can protect yourself from falling back into the old limiting behaviors and attitudes.

If you find yourself experiencing PGD, then it's time to climb out and get back to work. Utilize everything you have learned in this book and grab hold of the rope I just threw to you. Start the process of climbing out of the hole. I cannot pull you up. I can only throw you the rope. You have to take the action steps of climbing out of your own hole.

Take responsibility for yourself. You may wake up every day and take the world head on but people who are successful do it differently than everybody else. If you want to be part of the elite, then you must do what the elite do. Practice and apply these Universal Laws of the universe on a consistent daily basis. If you do this I guarantee something very special will happen.

CALL TO ACTION EXERCISE
1. Have an Exit Action Plan once you start getting close to accomplishing your goal [or if you come up short] so you don't run the risk of going through PGD.
2. If you are currently experiencing PGD, sit your ego down, let it throw its little temper tantrum and grab the rope I provided with this book and climb out. Don't worry. Ego will climb up after you. It can't stand being alone. You must continue your climb because you and your children's lives depend on it.

Chapter Ten

PATIENCE &
PERSISTENCE

*"Patience is waiting. Not passively waiting. That is
laziness. But to keep going when the going is hard
and slow – that is patience."*
— Unknown

We live in an instant gratification society. We want everything now. Unfortunately, there is a universal law called, *The Law of Gender*. It is the time it takes the seed you planted in the mind to germinate and manifest itself into your reality.

What would happen if we planted a seed and every day we dug it up to see if there was any progress? Would it survive? Probably not. If it did, it would take more time for it to germinate than if you would have just left it alone.

You do not want to disturb the seed. Your job is to make sure it gets ample sunshine, fertilizer and water in order to give it an environment for greatness. Then, you let the Universal Laws take over. Just because you can't see the germination of the seed unfold before

123

your eyes doesn't mean it's not working. All you can do is protect and nurture the environment and have faith in the beautiful laws of our universe.

We do the same thing with our own minds. We plant a goal and if we don't' perceive any progress then we give up. Have you ever heard of the gold miner who gave up on his goldmine too soon? He prospected his mine for months and months and grew tired of the effort. Another prospector offered to buy his tools and land. The deal was done. The new man hired experts to survey the land. They discovered that the first man was just THREE FEET from striking a huge deposit of gold.

There are many stories of highly influential and great people who have failed but never stopped persisting. Here are a few examples.

- *Henry Ford failed and went broke five times before he finally succeeded.*
- *Walt Disney was fired by a newspaper editor for lack of ideas. Disney also went bankrupt several times before he built Disneyland.*

- *Albert Einstein did not speak until he was four years old and didn't read until he was seven. His teacher described him as "mentally slow, unsociable and adrift forever in his foolish dreams." He was expelled and refused admittance to Zurich Polytechnic School. The University of Bern turned down his Ph.D. dissertation as being irrelevant and fanciful.*
- *The movie Star Wars was rejected by every movie studio in Hollywood before 20th-Century Fox finally produced it. It went on to be one of the largest grossing movies in film history.*
- *Michael Jordan was held back from the varsity basketball team when he was in 10th grade.*

Can you imagine if Henry Ford gave up? What about Albert Einstein or Walt Disney? I couldn't imagine not growing up without the *Star Wars* movies! What if Michael Jordan had quit after being denied a spot on the varsity team? Can you imagine basketball in the 80's and 90's without him? Right now, the next Albert Einstein, Walt Disney, Richard Branson or even the next great President of the United States may be sitting at your dinner table!

Football is not only a great game but it is a great teacher of life. I have learned and applied many of the lessons from this game to my own life and to that of my children. One of the most valuable lessons is persistence.

You fall down seven, you get up eight. (Japanese Proverb) You can have a great 99 yard drive and end up on the one yard line but if you don't punch it in for a score the drive means nothing to the outcome of the game. The fans don't remember the drive unless you score!

How many of us continue to be stuck on our own one yard line? We must have the guts and the tenacity to finish what we started and cross the goal line. You must never give up!

Sometimes you can make a change instantly in your mind and reap the benefits immediately as I did when I put my friend's glasses on. Sometimes it takes time. We must be patient and allow God to work His magic. I remember when I first started this process with my limiting belief on money. I used the affirmation, "I'm so happy and grateful now that money comes to me in increased quantities from multiple sources on a continued basis." On the first day I probably said it a hundred times. The next day I was at a gas station and as I was filling up my car I looked down and saw a dime. I started to laugh because I knew the affirmation worked. Many of you are probably thinking it is only a dime, but it is all relative (Law of Relativity). I knew in my heart and soul I attracted this little dime and I still have it to this day tucked away in my jewelry box as a reminder of how glorious this journey of self-discovery is.

The other day I was reminded of the lesson of patience when my older son was riding along with me to the grocery store on a country road. My mind was somewhere else and I didn't know I was driving with a heavy foot. My daydream was interrupted when I heard my son say, "Dad, I want to drive fast like you when I get bigger."

I instantly snapped back to reality, glanced down at my speedometer and noticed I was going way over the speed limit. I replied back to him, "Son, it is not okay to go fast on the highway. You must always follow the speed limit because this allows everybody to be safe on the road. Dad made a mistake and as you can see, I'm driving slower now. Thank you for reminding me to follow the speed limit."

Just like everything else, the way you drive is initially instilled in you by experiences while growing up. I started to reflect back on my childhood and how I perceived what proper driving was. A family member we'll call Joe, who has a very strong personality like me, was always in a rush when he drove. Every time we would travel he would try to make record time. I can't help but smile as I recall these stories which I will share with you.

One weekend, we were driving to visit my Nan. She lived an hour away and the country road to her house was filled with hills, curves and slow driving farmers. The speed limit was 55 mph and Joe would follow the speed limit around the curves but any straight away became the *Indianapolis 500*. Anybody who wasn't driving five mph over the speed limit was not following the "courtesy rules" of how to drive when somebody behind you is trying to break the record time to Grandma's house. If there was a person preventing Joe from achieving desired speed, he would follow this routine: First, he would get right on their tail and swerve back in forth to let them know he was there and he was not happy. Second, as soon as there was a chance to pass he would stomp the accelerator to the floor. It didn't matter if it was a no passing zone. As he would pass the other driver he would look at them and slowly shake his head back and forth with a disgusted look on his face. The final dagger in the heart of his "victim" would be him cutting them off. During this entire event, as we were all holding on for dear life, you would hear the familiar phrase, "Lead, follow, or get the hell out of the way."

Another instance, which I will never forget, was when Joe finally met his match—a 70 year old lady filled with pee and vinegar. It was a warm, sunny, peaceful Sunday morning with not a cloud in the sky. It was one of those days when you would look up to the blue sky and thank God to be alive. We were traveling down a two lane street where the speed limit was 25 mph. The town was empty and there was no one on the road except for us and Joe's new found arch nemesis. She was probably enjoying her peaceful morning until, Joe, a.k.a. Mario Andretti, was trying to make it home without anybody getting in his way. As he came up behind her, Joe followed his familiar "riding your butt" routine but things suddenly went sour when he went to pass and she cut him off. He tried again and she cut him off again. This woman, unbeknownst to him, was my new hero. Finally, after years of owning the roads like Mel Gibson in *Mad Max,* Joe had met his match. I was anxious to see how this new drama was going to turn out. This stubborn woman was not going to be bullied and was not going to back down. She was driving a big white pickup truck and we were sporting a small blue Pontiac 6000. It definitely was a David vs. Goliath matchup. I was rubbing my hands together thinking, "It is about to go down."

We swerved right and she bit and went right to block us but Joe floored the accelerator and went around to the left. We were now side by side going 60 mph, drag racing with a 70 year old woman with dentures clenched. I still remember him screaming, "Come on you old hag! I got you!"

Got her he did. He cut her off and now was in the lead. Now, his normal M.O. would be to speed off leaving his victim eating dust but this time I was in for a surprise. This time he had to prove a point to the old lady to never mess with the best. He slowed our vehicle down to a crawl.

Let's define what a "crawl" is. Have you ever just let your car slowly glide down a road without pushing on the accelerator? Well, Joe wasn't even doing that. In his mind, that was too fast. He had to use the brakes so the car would slowly inch forward. Then, he would swerve back and forth to prevent the old gal from passing. Next, he did something I will never forget. Joe turned around and started to wave and laugh at the woman whom he had just "conquered". I remember thinking, "Come on old gal, you have more in you,"

Oh, did she ever. I could hear her screaming, "You son-of-a-beep!"

The only thing that was louder than her screaming was Joe's laughter. After what felt like an eternity, which was probably only 10 seconds, he sped off to leave the beaten old woman to her defeat. He didn't say one word all the way home. He just drove home with a big old smile stretched from ear to ear.

These re-occurring high pressure driving lessons [on how to drive and how to be impatient] were established into me at a very young age. Without even realizing it, I was passing on my own horrible driving lessons to my son on how to drive fast and be an impatient driver. I didn't cut anybody off or have an ego battle with a 70 year old woman but it was still a negative lesson on how to drive poorly.

Analyze yourself and pinpoint the areas of your life where you feel impatient. It can be anything from driving, buying a house, losing weight, job promotion etc. When you feel impatient about anything you are letting your ego control your path. Impatience is working against God. Let your impatience, anxiety and stress go. Nothing good ever comes from experiencing any of these negative feelings. Remember you always have a choice on how to react to a situation and event. People who are successful on this journey do it differently. Be part of the elite and resonate high at all times.

CALL TO ACTION EXERCISE

1. If you are impatient it is time to change. I constantly work on my own impatience. We are in an instant gratification society and we must learn that once we plant seeds we must allow nature to do its part and allow the seed to grow. Impatience is like salting fertile ground. Some exercises I personally do to teach myself patience while driving is putting the cruise control on the posted speed limit and let everybody else pass me. In the beginning it was tough to let other people pass and "win" but I knew I was getting better when my anxiety wouldn't increase if somebody pulled out in front of me or cut me off.

2. When you find yourself thinking negative or feeling the negative feelings of anxiety, impatience, fear, worry, etc. take a deep breath and start to do your affirmations and visualization techniques and take back control of your mind.

Chapter Eleven

SCATTERING
YOUR ENERGY

---

*"Most people have no idea of the giant capacity we
can immediately command when we focus all of our
resources on mastering a single area of our lives."*
— **Anthony Robbins**

*"The successful warrior is the average
man, with laser-like focus."*
— **Bruce Lee**

*"Nothing can add more power to your life than concentrating
all your energies on a limited set of targets."*
— **Nido Qubein**

I was watching a program on the History Channel the other day about the cruise missile. What a remarkable and fantastic machine. It can be launched by ship, submarine, aircraft or even by a mobile ground launcher. After launch, the booster rocket is ejected. (Similar to what happens when the booster rockets separate from the space shuttle soon after launch.) Once the cruise missile loses its booster rocket the wings and tail fins unfold and the turbo-fan engine takes control. What makes this missile so incredible is that it has an onboard radar and terrain map, which allow it to precisely maneuver over terrain and around buildings. The onboard GPS guides the missile to the target and the Tercom (a navigation system used primarily by cruise missiles, that uses a pre-recorded contour map of the terrain that is compared to measurements made during flight by an on-board radar altimeter) and DSMAC (Digital Scene-Mapping Area Correlator, which is a combination of systems that allows pin point accuracy) pinpoint the target precisely. [7, 8]

It is truly remarkable to witness the flight pattern of this unmanned machine. It flies at very low altitude hugging the terrain and making adjustments along the way. If it doesn't get shot down, or if there is no mechanical failure, it always hits its target.

This is how you must approach any goal you want to achieve in your mind. When you instill a new goal into your mind you will have to make minor adjustments along the way. It usually isn't a straight road leading to your destination. There are hills, valleys, curves, road blocks, car crashes, bad weather, road kill, wind, hail, snow, rain, hurricanes, tornadoes....the point I am trying to make is that you will face challenges along the way. You must weather the storm and continue to your destination no matter what happens! Woody Hayes, a great college football coach from Ohio State, said *"Paralyze resistance with persistence."*

You also must have a clear and decisive plan of action for how you are going to achieve your goal. If you do not have a clear plan or destination your missile will miss its target.

An example of this is the *YouTube* phenomenon on "Leeroy Jenkins". The YouTube video features a group of players discussing a detailed battle strategy for the next encounter on a popular video game called *World of Warcraft* while one of their party members, Leeroy, is away from his computer. Their plan is ruined when Leeroy returns and, ignorant of the strategy, immediately charges headlong into battle shouting his own name in a stylized battle cry. His companions rush to help but Leeroy's actions ruin the meticulous plan and all of the group members are killed.[9]

One of the greatest self-destructive activities that interfere with our longevity of persistence is scattering our own energy. It is okay to have many goals that you want to achieve, but you can't do them all at once. I heard Oprah say, *"You can have anything and everything in this world, but not all at once."*

Let's go back to the farming example, since we are all farmers of the mind. Let's say we decide to grow some crops. The crops we have chosen to grow are corn, peas, beans, apples, walnuts, oranges, pineapples, potatoes and grapes.

What would happen if you mixed all these seeds together and put them in one small hole in the ground? Would they all grow? I guess some might, but wouldn't it make sense. If you want an abundance of a particular crop wouldn't you want it to grow in its own parcel? Being a country boy, I know there are some instances where you want to plant certain crops next to each other for nutrients but you would never plant them in the same hole. Imagine putting nine different kinds of seeds in the same hole. You probably wouldn't get an abundance of crops and the return on your investment would be minimal.

Even if you plant all of those different seeds in different holes you still would not have a plentiful crop if you scattered the water all around. You must concentrate on the seeds you want to grow first. Once they are established then you can venture out and plant different seeds.

We do the same thing in our minds. We have all these goals we want to achieve and if you do not structure them the right way you will scatter your energy. Remember your children are sponges and they will pick up this limiting activity if you are not aware. You must compartmentalize what you want to achieve first and go from there. You can't play in the NFL, NBA and in the Major Leagues all at once. There is not enough time to do all of these. I know there have been a few athletes who have achieved playing in multiple sports but it is very rare.

This was *me* early in my journey. I would try to accomplish all these things at once and I would continuously burn myself out and get frustrated when I was not attracting ultimate success. It wasn't until a good friend of mind took me aside and said, "You know what your problem is Garrett? You are good at everything. Everything you do you are successful at, but why don't you decide to be great at one thing?"

This really rang a bell of clarity in my mind. He was right. I was scattering all my energy at the time. It is okay to try to mimic the successes of people like Donald Trump, Richard Branson or music artists like Tim McGraw or Beyoncé but you can't be all these people at once. My point is this, decide on a goal you want to accomplish and do it. Then, build upwards from there. Each goal achieved, no matter if you perceive it to be great or small, will be another brick on your foundation. When you have enough solid bricks laid down you will have a solid foundation so you can build the skyscraper of your dreams.

What happens if you try to build a building too fast and don't let the mortar set? The building will crumble down along with not only your hard work but your hopes and your dreams. If this has happened to you in the past (I know it happened to me), or if it does happen in the future, you must REBUILD it the right way.

Do not try to do a million things at once. You will burn out and failure will always find you. If you continue to act out these same limiting behaviors over and over again you will find yourself very frustrated. Remember what Albert Einstein said about the definition insanity—doing the same thing over and over again expecting a different result.

We must train our minds, so we can train our children to focus their energy and mind. My father did just this. When I was in 8ᵗʰ grade he started to notice his younger son may have some talent to do something great. I was very good at two sports—football and baseball. He did what any great father did and built me a batting cage so I could sharpen my skills at the plate and a weight room in the basement so I could get bigger, faster and stronger. One year later, I batted over .500 my freshman year and I had a very successful season in football. He took me aside and said, "Son, I know you like to play both of these sports but which one will you be passionate about."

I thought for a moment and replied, "Football". The next day the batting cage was taken down and sold to a friend of ours.

He knew that if I was to be great at one, I had to give up the other. There is only so much energy you have. You can't play 75 games of baseball in the summer and expect to have enough energy left over to lift weights, run at the track and drag tractor tires up the hill. (Believe me, I tried.) You can't depend on a 9 volt battery to power a nuclear sub. You can try but your sub will sink to the bottom of the ocean. You must utilize all the available energy you have each day and you must not squander it. Don't get me wrong. I still played high school basketball and baseball but everyone knew my focus was football.

Now, are there athletes who are genetic freaks dominating all those sports in high school? Absolutely, but there are fewer of them who do it at the college level and at the professional level it is almost nonexistent.

There are people out there who have a "nuclear reactor" at their disposal to draw their energy from. I am one of these fortunate people. However, there are others who are only powered by a 9 volt battery. You must adapt your day to be as efficient as possible with the energy you have at your disposal. If you drain your battery too early then you won't have enough energy left over for the most important things in your life like your children and significant other. There are some days where I am guilty of this. I will go hard all day—starting at 5 a.m. to work out and then head off to the office to see my patients. The doors to my clinic open at 6:45 a.m. and I go all out trying to give my patients and the clients whom I coach my best until 7 p.m. (Some days I have speaking engagements which run past 9 p.m.) At the end of the day I try to draw the last amount of energy from my already spent reactor and be a great father to my two wonderful boys and passionate husband to my beautiful wife. There are some days when I finally lay down in bed and my wife looks at me with those beautiful brown eyes and suddenly I have the "headache". What does this do to the relationship when I deny her companionship and love? If there is not an open line of communication established in a relationship then there will be a gap between us. I may start the process of pouring cola into a new limiting belief in her mind that, "He doesn't love me and is not attracted to me anymore," even though it is not true. Sound familiar? We have to learn how to not squander our energy so that we have enough power left over for our family.

You must limit as many squandering activities as possible. For instance, you shouldn't set too many unrealistic goals. Another squandering activity would be allowing your ego to fly the plane called "worry" filled with the flight attendants serving the cool beverage of "fear". When you allow yourself to constantly be enveloped with the limiting feelings of worry and fear you are pulling the plug out of the bottom of the bathtub filled with your precious energy. Your energy will continuously pour down the drain until the bathtub is bone dry leaving you exhausted.

Other limiting activities include partying excessively and not getting enough sleep. We have all done this. How many times have you woken up in the morning after a long night of partying and found yourself saying, "I'm glad I drank so much last night."

I know I have never thought that. I usually moaned, "Why did I do this to myself?" You never get much done the next day when you are experiencing a hangover. It zaps all motivation, especially when you need to eat the triple cheeseburger and large fries to "soak up" the alcohol. All you end up with is feeling bloated. I don't know about you, but I have never looked at myself in the mirror after a night of drinking and eating cheeseburgers and said, "Wow, I'm one sexy man."

Doing these activities pours cola into your mind, which fuels the already established cancer of low self-esteem, holding you back from your goals and dreams.

This is why on some days you can do a million things and still feel as though you can run a marathon at the end of the day. Then there will be other days where you have done the same thing as before and feel as though you have nothing left and you are exhausted. The difference between the two days is you squandered your energy on one day and conserved your energy on the other. Everybody's energy level is different. This is why you just do the best with what God gave you. Just like I said before, you can't try to power a nuclear sub with a 9 volt battery. Utilize your energy to the best of your ability and everything else will fall into place.

CALL TO ACTION EXERCISE

1. You need to examine your life and filter out all the scattering activities which are taking time away from your most important

goals and more importantly, your family. Remember you can have everything and anything in this life—but not all at once.

2. If you start feeling worry and fear realize this is your ego and you are allowing it to control you. Put the "little maniac" in timeout and do your affirmations and visualization techniques as you have learned throughout the book.

Chapter Twelve

SERVICE

Service to others is the rent you pay
for your room here on earth.
—Muhammad Ali

Jesus called them together and said, "You know that those
who are regarded as rulers of the Gentiles lord it over them,
and their high officials exercise authority over them. Not so
with you. Instead, whoever wants to become great among you
must be your servant, and whoever wants to be first must be
slave of all. For even the Son of Man did not come to be served,
but to serve, and to give his life as a ransom for many.
—Mark 10:43-45 NIV[10]

I remember smiling when I read the story about how Marc Zuckerberg started *Facebook*. His intention was to create an open information flow for people. In essence, he was going to serve and serve he did. As of mid-2010, Facebook has reached the 500 million user mark. As of

2011 his personal wealth is estimated to be over $17.5 billion dollars. He was 27 years old.

When you serve people you are rewarded in some way. Think about any successful product. If it serves people it is successful. Usually, whoever is involved in the making and distributing of the product is rewarded financially. Facebook is no different. It serves people with the spread of knowledge. It has started revolutions—not only in other countries but within us. People now have the ability to share information at a moment's notice. I utilize it all the time in sharing the latest research on nutrition, pharmaceuticals and science. I also share motivational movies and quotes to allow people the opportunity to resonate high.

We must learn how to serve every day of our lives. We must everyday pay it forward. People tend to think they must tithe to serve. You do not have to give away all your money to serve (even though I tithe 10% of my own income to what I believe can make a difference). You can serve in other ways. When I am out in public I go out of my way to make sure everybody I come into contact will have my positive imprint left on them.

The other day my son Jack and I were shopping at *Meijer* (a local grocery store) and as we were walking to go inside I was picking up trash off of the ground and he was observing me (like our kids constantly do). I had the handful of trash I collected from the ground and I threw it away. When we got inside he asked, "Dad, why did you pick up all of that trash. It wasn't yours. Why did you pick it up?"

I bent down on one knee and replied, "When you see trash on the ground does it look nice?"

"No." was his reply.

I continued, "It is our responsibility to make this world a better and nicer place then we found it. How do we know that this isn't a test from God to see if we deserve nice things?" I always want to pass all of God's little tests because they add up to be big tests in this journey of life.

He shook his head in agreement and on the way out he went out of his way to pick up a plastic bottle and threw it in the garbage. He glanced at me with a big grin and gave me two thumbs up and yelled, "I passed the test Dad!"

I smiled and said a quiet prayer stating how grateful I was to be a father. You must teach your kids about service. When I was explaining to my great friend Ken about the activities I was doing with my two sons with their vision boards he brought up a valid point when he said, "Your son Jack's vision board is a great idea. You should have him earn a toy for his brother." I replied, "Genius, Ken!"

I went home and sat Jack down and asked him if he wanted to earn a toy for his brother because he was too little to do it for himself. He contemplated and replied, "Yeah dad, Alex likes trains. I will earn one for him."

Over the next 30 days Jack did his chores for his brother to earn a toy for him. He was even more excited than when he earned his own toy. When I saw Jack give Alex his new toy, I could see how proud of himself Jack was. You could see the bond between not only brothers but also between fellow human beings. I couldn't help but tear up when I witnessed how powerful we are as spiritual beings.

In *A Return To Love: Reflections on the Principles of A Course in Miracles,* Marianne Williamson hit the nail on the head when she said, *"Our deepest fear is not that we are inadequate. Our deepest fear is that we are powerful beyond measure.*

Every day you can decide to make a difference in not only your life but in the lives of everyone with whom you come in contact throughout the day. How hard is it to pass on a compliment or words of encouragement?

Just last Wednesday on my way to work, I was at a stoplight at 6:15 a.m. The gentleman next to me looked like he was going to have a long day. For some reason everybody always associates Wednesday to being the "hump day". Why is this? Yes, it is the middle of the week but why does Wednesday always have to be hard? It can be the best day of your life so far if you truly decide to make it happen. That morning, this other driver was obviously resonating "hump day" in every aspect of his being. His posture looked as if he was already a whipped dog. I decided to make a difference in his day. Now for those of you, who know me, you are probably smiling right now because you are probably thinking, "What are you going to do now, Dr. G."

I am a pretty big guy and I have one of those "Cheeeeeeese" smiles. I pulled up a little bit further so he could see me and I started to wave frantically trying to get his attention. He looked over with an expression of, "Who is this happy go lucky cheese ball?" I motioned him to roll down his window. He complied with hesitation and I hung out my window with two thumbs up and screamed, "Hey brotha, have a great freaken day! Shake and bake baby!"

He looked at me like I was on drugs and started to laugh as I drove off. I glanced in my rear view mirror and I saw he was still laughing. Now for those of you who think I am crazy, let's analyze what just happened. This guy was obviously going to have a "hump day". I interrupted his pattern and instilled a high energy one. I guarantee he went to work and for the rest of the day talked about this looney guy with a big cheese smile hanging out of his window, wishing him a great day. I'm sure everybody he tells the story to will get a chuckle. This starts a ripple effect, which will carry across the planet. Maybe instead of going home to his wife and kids in a bad mood, as he usually does every Wednesday, he now will go home in a great mood resonating his sincere love towards them. How do you think his kids will like the new "Wednesday night" dad? Maybe he will make passionate love to his wife like he hasn't done in a long time, showing her how much love he still has for her. Maybe this guy was contemplating suicide and this one act of crazy kindness was a glimmer of hope, which will allow him to get on the right path. You never know what small act you may do that will change somebody for the better.

The other day my family and I went to the grocery store to buy some groceries for a party we were having. Thinking I was only going to be a couple of minutes I had my wife and younger son wait for us in the car. I walked in with my oldest son and the store was packed full of people. I thought to myself, "Well, this is what I get for coming to the store on a Saturday."

We walked past the carts and my son said, "Dad you need a cart."

I looked down and flexed by arm and replied, "Who needs a cart when you have these guns baby."

He started to laugh and we continued our mission to get our supplies for the party. As we bobbed and weaved throughout the busy store acquiring all of our groceries I started to notice we were compiling too many supplies to carry. I had 2 boxes of beer and pop in both hands and my son was toting a case of water and chips. Needless to say we were both showing signs of fatigue. We finally finished shopping and made our way towards the checkout line and looked down at my son and said, "We are almost there bud."

When I saw the long line you could tell Jack was frustrated when he said, "We should have gotten a cart muscle dad."

I looked down and laughed, "Touché' son."

As were waiting, a young woman in her forties had a cart full of groceries. She glanced back at us and probably noticed the sweat on my face and the frustration on my sons face because she said, "Why don't you and your son go in front of me."

I replied, "Ma'am, thank you, but you don't have to do that. We will wait our turn."

She smiled and said, "It appears you will be entertaining guest and you look like you are in a hurry. Just go in front of me because I have a cart full of groceries and it will take forever for me to get checked out."

I looked down at my son and he was giving me the "Take the offer" expression. I looked at this woman and with sincerity replied, "Thank you so much for being so generous. We really appreciate it."

As we were walking by the young lady humorously said, "All you have to do it pay for my groceries."

We both started to laugh and as I was getting checked out, I looked at the young girl working the cash register and I told her to put all of the woman's groceries on my credit card.

You should have seen the look on her face. It was if all the air was sucked right out of her lungs. She immediately started to say, "Please, you don't have to do this. You can't do this. I was only kidding."

Which I replied with a smile, "I wasn't kidding."

She started to cry and through her tears she said, "Thank you so much. I really needed this."

I smiled and replied, "No, it is I who am thankful for you. You were very generous in letting me go in front of you, which is why you should be rewarded. This is what life is about."

I paid her bill and went on my way. The best part of this interaction was my son got to witness the entire event. I knew I did the right thing when I heard him look up at me and say, "Dad, someday I'm going to do that too."

I knelt down and explained to him we are on this planet to serve as many people as we can and you will never know how one small act of kindness may change somebody's life for the better. Just like Muhammad Ali said, *"Service to others is the rent you pay for your room here on earth"*.

Every time I am interacting with society I try to leave my positive imprint on everyone I come into contact with. It can be as small as a compliment on a piece of clothing to how nice their smile is. Imagine if everyone did this? How much better would this world be? Imagine if you taught your kids to do this?

CALL TO ACTION EXERCISE

1. Are you now starting to see what God truly wants us to accomplish as spiritual beings living a human experience? After finishing this book, go out and make a difference. Not tomorrow, but now! Go to your children, pick them up and tell them how much you love them. Find your significant other and passionately kiss them like you haven't done in a long time. Call your mom and dad or whoever raised you and tell them how much you appreciate everything they have done for you. Compliment a complete stranger. Take every negative situation that has happened to you in the past and turn it into a positive experience. When faced with a negative situation in the future always remember you have a choice on how you respond to it. Resonate high people and live the life God intended for you to live. A life filled with meaning and passion. You can and will make a difference!

It began with a thought....

EPILOGUE

Throughout life there will always be doubters, haters, negative people, etc. If you continue to live your life by everybody else's standards then you will live a very limited life. Take control right now! Stand up and proclaim, "*This is who I am! This is what I'm about! I'm going to take control of my life and live the life I dream of and nothing and nobody will stand in my way!*"

As you've probably already noticed, this book was about training parents to stop limiting their children with their own limiting thoughts and actions. For our children to be successful in this journey we call life they need to be loved, disciplined, have established boundaries, listened to, guided, respected, hugged, kissed, loved, loved and loved.

When I first thought of writing this book, my own ego reared up and said, "You can't write. Nobody will buy this book. You are in the beginning of fatherhood. What proof do you have that this will work. You are going to look stupid. You don't make any sense."

I initially felt fear and nervousness, but I squashed those feelings immediately. I reaffirmed in my own mind why I wanted to finish this book. The reason being is the vision I have for all the children. I truly believe we are in a very dangerous time and if we do not change our thinking on a variety of things, life on this earth will cease to exist as we know it.

Will we see this vision come into fruition in our own lives? There is a slim possibility. A vision is always pursued, and never attained, but it leaves a legacy for others to continue. I may not live long enough for my vision to come into my reality but I will leave my fossilized footprint for others to follow down the path of the next Golden Age of our species.

I would like to first thank my beloved wife Jennifer. Honey, you will never know what you mean to me. You are my foundation for our skyscraper of everlasting love. You are my soul mate and I adore you. Thank you for always supporting me and being there with me to support me through the bad times and celebrate our good times. Because of you, I am where I am today. I look forward to holding your hand as we travel down our path together.

To my two beautiful sons, Jack and Alex. I will always be there for you and you will never know how much your mother and I love you until the day you witness your own children coming into this world. To be the best! Not what other people want you to do, but always strive to be YOUR best at whatever you will be passionate about in your life.

Mom, you have always been there for me. You have always been there to listen, give a hug when I needed it most and always there to turn my frown into a smile. Everybody who knows you is well aware that God definitely broke the mold when he made you. You mean so much to this world and everybody you touch. Thank you for being there mom and loving me.

Dad, thanks for instilling leadership, dedication, hard work, drive, persistence and all the other qualities that make up a great father, entrepreneur and business man. Thank you for always being in my corner and believing in me.

To my man Butch, thank you for instilling the Universal Laws and "hot tub philosophy" into my mind at such a young age. "B & G" my man, enough said.

Ken Collard, thank you for all your guidance, input and most importantly your love for humanity. It is men like you who make a positive difference in the world. Thank you for what you do.

To Evelyn (I know you will kill me for using your real name ☺) and the rest of the Carlisle clan, thanks for enriching my family's life. You are the definition of persistence. Your experiences as a family will always leave a great imprint in my mind on how to raise and love your children, no matter what perceived challenges happen along your path. I am grateful our paths crossed.

To my mother-in-law Betty, thank you for all the love and guidance you had throughout my journey writing this book. It meant the world to me.

To all of my Bronco Brothers with whom I have bled, sweat and shed tears through our time playing football at "The Western Michigan University." All of you will always be my brothers and nobody can ever take away the camaraderie we have with one another. "Say Now, Bronco Brothers!"

To all my Wellness Families, with whom I interact every day. It has been truly an honor and I am grateful to serve all of you. Your commitment to your family's health has been an inspiration and reaffirms why I became a Chiropractor.

I would like to thank all the people who will apply the teachings you have learned here and will change humanity for the better. You all are the true heroes and I am grateful to serve you.

Lastly, I would like to thank God for the abundance he has showered over my life. I am eternally grateful and humble to be able to serve.

With sincere love and gratitude,
Garrett L. Soldano

ABOUT THE AUTHOR

Garrett Soldano describes a definite science to being a successful parent, built on a foundation of his life experiences growing up in poverty and witnessing two very young parents, completely raw in their skills, living in a trailer park, who still succeeded in pulling themselves from poverty, while providing their sons the necessary prerequisites to move forward in life. It is here where he began to study, formalize, and apply the lessons of Universal Laws to athletics, entrepreneurship and parenting. Mr. Soldano is also a motivational speaker and has regular video blogs on "God's True Law" on Facebook and www.Godstruelaw.com.

He resides in Mattawan, Michigan with his wife and two sons.

REFERENCES

1. "Belief." 2011. In Merriam-Webster.com. Retrieved May 8, 2011, from http://www.merriam-webster.com/dictionary/Belief.

2. "Which of you, if his son asks for bread, will give him a stone?" (Matthew 7:9 New International Version 1984).

3. "Bear with each other and forgive whatever grievances you may have against one another. Forgive as the Lord forgave you." (Colossians 3:13 New International Version 1984).

4. Swanson, J.M., et al. "Effect of stimulant medication on children with attention deficit disorder: a review of reviews," *Exceptional Children*, 60:154-62, 1993.

5. Smith S.E. (2003). What is Crab Mentality. Retrieved June 17, 2011, from www.wisegeek.com/what-is-the-crab-mentality.htm.

6. "Goal." 2011. In Merriam-Webster.com. Retrieved August 10, 2011, from http://www.merriam-webster.com/dictionary/Goal.

7. "Cruise Missile." In Wikipedia.com. Retrieved May 20, 2011, from http://en.wikipedia.org/wiki/Cruise_missile.

8. "Cruise Missile." In Howstuffworks.com Retrieved May 20. 2011, from http://science.howstuffworks.com/cruise-missile3.htm.

9. "Leeroy Jenkins." In Wikipedia.com. Retrieved September 17, 2011, from http://en.wikipedia.org/wiki/Leeroy_Jenkins.

10. "Jesus called them together and said, "You know that those who are regarded as rulers of the Gentiles lord it over them, and their high officials exercise authority over them. Not so with you. Instead, whoever wants to become great among you must be your servant, and whoever wants to be first must be slave of all. For even the Son of Man did not come to be served, but to serve, and to give his life as a ransom for many." (Mark 10:43-45 New International Version 1984).